MIWOK MEANS PEOPLE

MIWOK
Means People

The life and fate
of the native inhabitants
of the California Gold Rush country.

Eugene L. Conrotto

1973
VALLEY PUBLISHERS
FRESNO, CALIFORNIA

STANDARD BOOK NUMBER: 0-913548-13-8

LIBRARY OF CONGRESS CATALOG CARD NUMBER: 72-96689

COPYRIGHT © 1973 BY VALLEY PUBLISHERS

Dedication

This book is for my son,
DUANE LAWRENCE CONROTTO
who has, among his many fine attributes,
compassion for his fellow man.

Picture Credits

We acknowledge with appreciation the courtesy extended us by the following:

Lowie Museum of Anthropology, University of California, for pictures on pages 6, 15 (4), 49, 51, 52 (2), 54, 55, 56, 57, 61, 63, 68 (2), 70, 75, 85 (left), and 88 (2).

Department of Parks and Recreation, State of California, for pictures on pages 19, 21, 26, 47, 48, 49, 84, 85 (right), and 89.

California State Library for pictures on pages 2, 5, 35, 53, 67, 86 (2), 93, 97, and 99.

About the Author

Eugene L. Conrotto is a native of northern California (Gilroy) and a graduate of Stanford University. He and his wife, Jeanne, spent nearly a year in Miwok country in the Angels Camp area, and then moved to Southern California, where he spent nearly ten years with *Desert Magazine,* rising from associate editor to editor and finally to publisher of that nationally-known regional publication.

While at *Desert,* Conrotto spent much time and wrote many articles on the Indians of the Southwest, particularly the Hopi, Utes and Navajo. The latter tribe provided Conrotto with the opportunity to assist Gilbert Maxwell write his highly successful *Navajo Rugs,* now in its 19th printing.

After his stint at *Desert,* Conrotto remained in that area to found and edit the *Palm Desert Post.*

In 1967 the Conrottos returned to Miwok country -- this time across the Stanislaus River two miles south of Columbia, where they purchased a ranch on historic Mormon Creek. Conrotto then returned to college -- Stanislaus State -- and received his general secondary credential, and is currently working on his master's degree in English. He has been a teaching assistant at Stanislaus State and is a full-time teacher of English and communications at Oakdale High School.

Conrotto's book *Lost Desert Bonanzas,* published in 1964, is regarded as one of the most important works in that genre.

The Conrottos have one son, Duane, a student at Columbia Junior College.

Table of Contents

MIWOK MEANS PEOPLE

1

In The Beginning

Their word for "person" was "miwu", and so the white man said they were properly the plural of person, "the people" -- "Miwok".

It took some doing at that. The literature reveals a variety of spellings: Mewahs (1856), Meewa (1873), Meewie (1873), Meewoc (1873), Miwa (1877), Miwi (1877), Miwok (1877), Miook (1885), and Muwa (1904). (The Tuolumne County Library, in the very heart of Miwok country, carries its card catalog reference as Mewuk, a spelling not to be found in serious print, the lone exception being the unpublished manuscripts of anthropologist C. Hart Merriam, who described some "Mewuk" ceremonials witnessed in 1906. But Merriam's editors make reference throughout this work to the "Miwok".)

More often than not, the white man simply lumped the Miwok and their neighbors into a non-existent "tribe" he called "Digger". This unfortunate name came from the fact these native California people used digging sticks to harvest bulbs and tubers. It is a pity the name-givers did not follow the harvest home to study how the harvester shared it with whatever guest came to his door. Perhaps the white man then would have called him a "Sharer" or even a "Giver".

But "Digger Indian" was not the worst of the brands burned into the flesh of these peaceable people. All American Indians, of course, were "savages" and "pagans" by common agreement among the whites, but the 19th Century frontier scholar measured the Miwok against the other American native peoples and found he had not yet "achieved" that level of tribal development marked by the "ability to conduct war for plunder". From this he concluded the Miwok was a "primitive" -- stone-age vintage.

Twentieth Century man, driven to categorize and classify everything in the universe and beyond, divided the Miwok into three segments:

--Lake Miwok lived on the shores of Clear Lake;

--Coast Miwok occupied the shoreline of Marin County (Sir Francis Drake spent the summer of 1579 with the Coast Miwok. Various Miwok words and phrases occur in the records of the Drake voyages); and

--Interior Miwok of the Sierra Nevada Mountains and foothills.

1

When Sir Francis Drake landed in California he discovered the Coast Miwok north of San Francisco Bay. The caption for this illustration in Soules Annals of San Francisco *reads: "The King of California places his crown of feathers on Admiral Drake's head."*

The Coast and Lake Miwok were Miwok in origin more than in fact. That is, culturally they had become more similar to their San Francisco Bay Area neighbors, while their interior-dwelling cousins, less influenced by neighbors because of space, remoteness and terrain, remained more purely Miwok.

The Interior Miwok occupied the very heart of California. Their wedge-shaped territory stretched from the delta country between Sacramento and Stockton eastward and southward into the great Sierra.

The white man further separated these Interior Miwok into four sub-groups: Plains, Northern, Central and Southern -- estimating that in pre-Caucasian times each separate interior dialect numbered about 2000 souls, and the combined dialects numbered about 9000.

The Plains Miwok lived along the low country adjacent to the Sacramento River. They were the "wealthy" Miwok because their environment was rich with waterfowl, delta vegetation, and deep-water fish. They lived in tule-thatched houses, used tule balsas to navigate the waterways, and developed advanced fishing equipment. Their generous

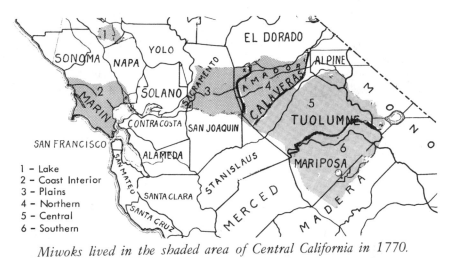

1 - Lake
2 - Coast Interior
3 - Plains
4 - Northern
5 - Central
6 - Southern

Miwoks lived in the shaded area of Central California in 1770.
habitat provided them with a life-style markedly different from that of their
poorer foothill cousins, and for 4000 to 20,000 years -- depending on the
school of anthropology to which you subscribe, but certainly from at least
the time of Christ -- the Sacramento River dwellers were the "lucky"
Miwok. And then -- with the swiftness of a plow breaking the incredibly
fertile delta soil -- these people became the "unlucky" Miwok. Next day
they were gone: obliterated, forgotten. The white man had come!

Northern, Central and Southern Miwok, the true foothill people, were
culturally similar. The slight variations that existed between them were
due to influences of their respective non-Miwok neighbors.

We shall refer to these three groups from this point forward collectively
as the "Sierra Miwok" or simply the "Miwok". This book is about these
people.

They occupied the grass-covered, sometimes bushy, but comparatively
open foothills of the Sierra Nevada which extend eastward into the wooded
mountains. On the lower elevations they lived in grass-thatched houses.
Higher up, the building material was barkslab. There were few cultural
differences from north to south within a given altitude range through the
entire Sierra Nevada territory.

Truly these people were one, and as one they felt the full impact of one
of history's most momentous migrations: the California Gold Rush.

The Sierra Miwok territory falls almost exactly within the boundaries of
the Mother Lode's great Southern Mines.

For a brief period -- perhaps two decades -- there were up to 100,000
white men (a ratio of nearly 20 white men to every Miwok) bent on
turning over every Miwok stone in search of gold. Fortunately, the gold
gave out before the Miwoks, and most of the gold hunters pounded their

3

way back to San Francisco or over the mountains to Nevada's silver fields.

The Miwok -- 670 of them according to the 1910 census -- were saved. They stole away to higher, less hospitable ground where their blood flows to this day.

The three Sierra Miwok dialect settlements generally follow the drainage patterns of the gold-bearing rivers that run westward out of the Sierra.

The Northern Miwok lived along the Cosumnes, Mokelumne and Calaveras Rivers. Here today are the towns of Jackson, Mokelumne Hill, San Andreas, Volcano, Railroad Flat and West Point.

The Central Miwok occupied the Stanislaus and Tuolumne River drainages. In this territory today are Sonora, Columbia, Jamestown, Twain Harte, Tuolumne City, Chinese Camp, and Mi-Wuk (note especially) Village.

The Southern Miwok lived along the Merced, Mariposa, Chowchilla and Fresno Rivers. Mariposa is the largest modern town in this region. However, its crowning glory is Yosemite Valley, the archetypical Indian paradise -- Miwok country -- the eden which these people left absolutely unspoiled.

On the floor of the San Joaquin Valley, from modern Stockton south through Modesto, Manteca, Fresno, Tulare and Bakersfield -- along the long westward foot of the Miwok's Sierra -- lived the Yokuts.

The Maidu flanked the Miwok on the north and occupied the foothills and higher reaches of the Sierra from the Cosumnes River and modern Sacramento to Mt. Lassen and modern Susanville and including Quincey, Downieville, Grass Valley, Colfax, Marysville, Oroville, Chico and Placerville.

Behind the Miwok, eastward across the Sierra, lived the Washo and Mono.

The Miwok knew no such formal tribal designations. Humanity -- Miwok and otherwise -- stretched from their Sierra domain endlessly in all directions. To the people of one village, those of another to the north were simply ''northerners''. Of course, these ''northerners'' were ''southerners'' to those north of them.

The Miwok had only one generic name for a group of foreigners -- ''Keyuew-k'' -- ''salt people'' -- for the Indians the white man called ''Mono'', and from whom the Miwok obtained salt.

If modern scientists can catalog people into tribes and divide tribes into dialect divisions, so too can they group several tribes into ''families'' or ''nations'' or even into all-encompassing ''empires''.

Thus, the Miwoks make up one-fifth of the so-called Penutian Empire which occupied nearly half of California -- a very diverse piece of real estate.

*One of the first newspaper illustrations of Miwok life. This engraving is of
the Miwok village on Dry Creek near its junction with the Mokelumne
River. The artist captured the scene "a short time previous to the dif-
ficulties narrated" -- armed whites, suspecting the Indians here of
stealing, drove them from their homes. The year: 1853.*

The Penutians include the Wintun (Sacramento Valley), Maidu
(northern Sierra), Miwok (central Sierra), Costanoans (San Francisco Bay
area south to Monterey) and Yokuts (San Joaquin Valley).

It is of more than passing significance that more than 100 languages and
dialects were spoken by the natives of California when the white man first
arrived on the scene. There were 21 distinct families of languages (some
authorities reduce this figure to seven), each of which is regarded as
coordinate in rank with the great Indo-European language family, which
includes English, Sanskrit, German, Latin and a host of other tongues.

Such an aggregation of languages within so limited a geographic area as
California is not found anywhere else in the world.

Add to this the fact that California had an estimated native population of
between 100,000 and 150,000 -- one of the most densely populated
regions of the pre-Columbian Western Hemisphere -- a full eighth of the
entire native population in what is now the United States -- and we come
to the realization that the Miwok and his neighbors were above all else
peaceful; they simply did not impose their way of life on others.

The white man, using his incredibly lopsided scale of values, interpreted this lack of desire to conquer or to spread culture by force as
evidence of "cultural morbidity". In the face of this lack of understanding
on the part of the white man, who was ever ready to reinforce his beliefs
with gunpowder, his self-imposed obligation to Christianize the world and
later his rampant "pursuit of happiness". the Miwok and his California
neighbors did not have a chance.

5

Miwok country. The middle fork of the Tuolumne River near Wards Ferry. Photographed by E. W. Gifford in July, 1913.

2

The Setting

California has always been a land of allure.

It was brought into history by the popular Spanish novelist Montalvo when he wrote: "Know ye that at the right hand of the Indies there is an island called California, very close to that part of the Terrestrial Paradise, which was inhabited by black women without a single man among them, and they lived in the manner of Amazons. They were robust of body with strong, passionate hearts and great virtue. The island itself is one of the wildest in the world on account of its bold and craggy rocks."

For the next 300 years California remained, to the European world, a distant fabled shangri-la, peopled perhaps not by giants but by what had still to be a fabulous race.

In the 18th Century the Spaniards, to meet the challenge of the Alaska-based Russians, moved a thin colonizing finger north from Mexico to San Francisco Bay. By 1840, however, it was generally conceded that the California region was going to be owned eventually by either France, England or the United States. The latter succeeded, though not without vigorous opposition from the Mexicans and even some Americans.

Daniel Webster, the great northern Senator, was not impressed with the romantics' long-running love affair with the sunset land. "What do we want with this vast worthless area?...this region of savages and wild beasts, of deserts of shifting sands and whirlwinds of dust, of cactus and prairie dogs? To what use could we ever hope to put these great deserts, or those endless mountain ranges, impenetrable and covered to their very base with eternal snow?"

It is obvious that the idea of a "fabulous race" in California no longer existed in the popular mind on the eve of the gold miners' invasion.

The 1848 gold rush galvanized the world's attention on the foothill lands of the Maidu and Miwok.

This was the world's first international gold rush, and to the Sierra came many men and a few women from all corners of the globe.

From the American east they came by ship to San Francisco and then inland to the mines. From the midwest and south they came overland, braving deserts and angry natives. They came from the Hawaiian Islands, from Australia, from Germany, Sweden, France, Italy, Russia and England. The exotic Chinese were imported to build a railroad over the mountains, and then turned loose to fend for themselves in the gold fields. The Mexicans, whose land this had been, drifted northward into the Sierra. (In the summer of 1849, as many Mexicans settled in a single Miwok-territory community, Sonora, as there were Miwoks on the entire face of the earth!) Chilean miners, Jewish merchants, Irish roustabouts and French whores hurried to the mountains to seek their fortunes.

This generally young, always vigorous and patently self-centered crowd provided California with a foundation stock that gave future generations an outward tolerance for variety -- at least amongst people of their own skin color.

California, with its lack of summer rains, was a different kind of world to most of the gold seekers, more used to a countryside white in winter and green in summer.

California summers are dry and brown and, in the days when transportation depended on alfalfa and grass, noticeably lacking in natural food.

This land received mixed reviews from these first observers. There is a noticeable lack of mention of the land's native population.

"One of the queerest things I know of," wrote Mark Twain, "is to hear tourists from the States go into ecstasies over the loveliness of 'ever-blooming California'. And they always do go into that sort of ecstasies. But, perhaps they would modify them if they knew how old Californians, with the memory full upon them of the dust-covered and questionable summer greens of California 'verdure', stand astonished, and filled with worshiping admiration, in the presence of the lavish richness, the brilliant green, the infinite freshness, the spendthrift variety of form and species and foliage that make an Eastern landscape a vision of Paradise itself...No land with an unvarying climate can be very beautiful."

The Sierra Nevada range rises gradually from the floor of the Great Central Valley to 10,500-foot peaks which fall away sharply, generally along the Nevada line, to form a perpendicular barrier facing east.

From the valley floor to the summits, varying in distance from 40 to 70 linear miles, are a half-dozen life zones. The Miwok lived in the lower three. Above 4000 feet the Sierra winters are too snowy for people to live without modern shelter. The Indians who frequented this higher ground did so only on short hunting or food-gathering forays. Yosemite is in this highest-third Miwok zone. It was a summer resort of the adjacent Miwok, and also to parties of Washo and Mono, who came from the east to trade. A few Miwok lived in Yosemite the year around.

Then, as now, the bulk of the Sierra dwellers lived in the two lower life zones.

Moving from the Valley floor to the summits, this first foothill zone is known as the Lower Sonoran Zone, a region characterized as "hot steppe". Its upper elevation is 1000 feet. Here we find open waters -- rivers and sloughs -- marshes, meadows, hog-wallow prairies, rose thickets and rock outcrops.

On the river bottoms of the Lower Sonoran Zone of the east side of the San Joaquin Valley grow Fremont cottonwoods and valley oaks. The community of Snelling, at an elevation of 250 feet, is a representative point in this life zone. Here thrived mockingbird, Texas nighthawk, blue grosbeak, dwarf cowbird, Fresno pocket gopher, Merced kangaroo rat and golden beaver.

Principal food animals trapped and hunted by the Miwok who lived in this life zone were antelope, jackrabbit, ducks, geese, salmon and grasshoppers. Houses and women's skirts were made of tule; blankets were created out of feathers and rabbit-skin. Deerskins were used extensively in their dress.

Modern localities in this life zone are Ione, Knight's Ferry, La Grange and Merced Falls.

The Upper Sonoran Zone ("Hot Summer Mediterranean") was home to most of the Miwok, just as today it has the greatest population density in the Sierra. Jackson, Campo Seco, Angels Camp, Jamestown, Sonora, Columbia, Springfield, Coulterville, Baxter, Hornitos, Hite Cove and El Portal are located in this belt.

The elevation range is 1000 to 3000 feet (4000 feet on south-facing slopes). The landscape is characterized by streams, meadows, dry grasslands, rocky slopes and vegetation that includes digger pines, buckeyes, blue oaks, interior live oaks and chaparral.

Distinctive birds are the California jay, northern brown townee, pallid wren-tit, plain titmouse, California thrasher, California bush-tit, San Joaquin wren, Hutton vireo, Anna hummingbird, western gnatcatcher, Bell sparrow, rufous-crowned sparrow, dusky poor-will and Nuttal woodpecker. Here, too, live the Mariposa brush rabbit, Gilbert white-footed mouse, parasitic white-footed mouse, digger pine pocket gopher, Heermann kangaroo rat, San Diego alligator lizard, and California striped racer.

The Miwok here lived in houses covered with the bark of the digger pine. He hunted deer, jackrabbit and valley quail.

Miwok residence sites within the third or Transition Zone ("Intermediate Mediterranean") were not numerous. Here we find swift streams, meadows, dry grasslands, boulder-talus slopes and cliffs. Today's

Mokelumne Hill, West Point, Tuolumne City, Murphys, Yosemite, Mariposa and Oakhurst are in this zone.

As with Yosemite, this summer resort land has a warm-weather appeal, but we must not have the impression that the Miwok traveled hither and yon throughout the Sierra trying to find a breath of cool air in the summer, or a warm patch of sunshine in winter. Rare was the Miwok who, in his lifetime, journeyed more than 20 miles from home. And it is undoubtedly true that there were some Miwok women who lived their entire lives and were then buried or burned within sight and sound of the place of their birth.

The Miwok who lived in the Transition Zone covered his house with yellow pine bark or the Sequoia Big Tree. He captured and ate deer, gray squirrel, Mountain quail, pigeons, trout and chrysalids. He got his salt by trade from the Monos. His blankets were made of fur. His women made skirts from grass and deerskins.

The blue-green of the digger pine yields to the deeper green of the western yellow pine, providing a distinctive boundary line between the Transition and the Upper Sonoran zones. Other distinctive Transition Zone trees are the Douglas spruce, golden oak, black oak and incense cedar.

The wildlife in this third zone is markedly different than that of lower elevations. Here we find the band-tailed pigeon, California purple finch, black-throated gray warbler, Calaveras warbler, western flycatcher, black swift, pigmy owl, northern spotted owl and the northwestern long-legged bat. Mammals include the Boyle white-footed mouse, Yosemite pocket gopher, and coral king snake.

The 6000-foot contour generally marks the start of fourth or Canadian life zone. This is a land of swift streams and granite outcrops. The golden oak gives way to the dwarf huckleberry oak. The California laurel and maple and black oak disappear. Yellow pine is replaced by the Jeffrey pine. Red firs and aspens appear. The characteristic birdlife includes Yosemite fox sparrow, Williamson sapsucker, Sierra grouse, red-breasted nuthatch and the California evening grosbeak. On the ground are the navigator shrew, Allen jumping mouse, yellow-haired porcupine, Sierra mountain beaver, Tahoe chipmunk and the Tenaya (remember that name) lizard.

Just below timberline is the fifth or Hudsonian Zone and its lodgepole pine, Alpine hemlock, silver pine and white-bark pine. Here we have lakes, heather and rock slides. While mammals remain plentiful, there is a thinning-out of birds in this zone: California pine grosbeak, mountain bluebird and white-crowned sparrow. This is the home of the Alpine Chipmunk, Belding ground squirrel, Sierra marmot, mountain lemming mouse, gray bushy-tailed wood rat, Yosemite cony, Sierra white-tailed jackrabbit, pine marten, wolverine and Sierra least weasel.

The Arctic-Alpine, sixth and highest of all life zones, ranges above timberline (about 10,500 feet). The Sierra Nevada rosy finch is the only species of bird confined to this zone, but some of the Hudsonian mammals enter it locally. We can be sure this zone, and to only slightly lesser degrees the Hudsonian and Canadian zones immediately below it, held little or no appeal to the Miwok. Like the ancient Greek who sang the praises of the sea but clung to the dry land, the Miwok no doubt thrilled to the sight of the eastern mountain peaks crowned with the year's first snow, but he remained planted in the sunshine and warmth of his foothill home.

Although residence in a particular life zone was the chief determinant of a Miwok's material culture, he was not prevented from enjoying some of the blessings obtainable at another level.

Thus, Upper Sonoran Zone people visited the valley floor to hunt antelope or trade for salmon. Transition Zone mountain people moved into the Canadian Zone in summer to gather sugar pine nuts.

Moving from one life zone to another was not, in most cases, an involved undertaking. Transition Zone Miwok who lived near the steep deep canyons of the Stanislaus, Tuolumne and other rivers were but an hour's climb down the canyon walls to the Upper Sonoran flora and fauna at the canyon bottoms. The Miwok in the higher elevations almost always built their villages near a spring or stream on the edge of the river canyons for this very reason. In the Lower Sonoran Zone the Miwok did live near the rivers, whose canyon walls here are not steep.

The Miwok was tied to his Sierra environment by his food quest, and he was a pure harvester -- he neither planted crops nor herded livestock. When the Spanish and Mexican colonizers of the coastal and valley areas introduced horses to California, the Miwok remained a peaceable, food-gathering people and simply treated this animal as a new source of meat (preferring it to beef). Similarly, the horse allowed the Plains Indians and the Apaches and Navajo of the Southwest, who were already predators (that is, they lived by raiding), to become more mobile, and hence more dangerous, predators -- the "greatest light cavalry on earth". The horse did not change the basic way of life, either for the Plains Indians or the Miwoks.

The Miwok, locked into his cultural patterns, had no need for easy transportation, even to expand the boundaries of his harvest grounds to secure more food. The horse was eaten because it was the answer to the problem at hand -- the problem of finding a substitute for the rabbits, deer, bears and other animals killed and eaten by the hordes of white men.

"And here's a different one," Miwok informant Castro Johnson told

11

University of California investigators. "Long ago the Indians used to go to the west to get horses, to steal them. When they came back, they stole them and used to bring the horses of the Mexicans. Then they were chased and tracked up these mountains. Then two old men were reached by these Mexicans, who made war on them and kept on shooting at them.

"They shot one old man's bowstring. But then he dodged around, it didn't matter that his bowstring was shot off.

"They kept on shouting for their comrades, yelling. Then their comrades saw them from on top of the mountain. They ran down and chased them. They fought each other back and forth.

"Then these Mexicans got scared and went west, they went home. Then one man chased them, up the hill they went. Way up on top he got to them. But nobody got killed. Then they went back, these Mexicans, to their houses there in the west. But they didn't take any of the horses, they didn't take them back. All of their horses were killed and made into meat. So! That's all."

3

Who The Miwok Were

Like most other peoples everywhere, the Miwok have a story of how the world came to be.

Before the People were created, there were six different races in the world. The first were like the People. After they had lived on earth a long time, the great cannibal giant, Uwulin, came down from the north eating the humans he could catch and place in the hunting sack slung over his back.

Uwulin soon had eaten nearly all the first people, and he lay down to sleep.

The few remaining people gathered to make a plan to kill the giant. They sent Fly to examine the killer. Fly started at Uwulin's head and bit him on every part of his body, but the giant slept on. Finally, Fly bit him on the heel, and the giant jerked his foot and kicked.

Fly returned to the people and told them of his discovery. They held a council and decided to place a great many large bone awls on the trail.

When the giant awoke, he ambled down the trail looking for human food. He stepped on a sharp awl and was killed.

Uwulin died near the present town of Coulterville where his petrified bones were found some years ago. The man who dug up these huge bones died within a few days of his desecration.

The second race of people were the Bird people. They, too, had their nemesis: the spirit Yelelkin, who stole most of the people. And then the earth was overrun by giant black ants, and the remaining people left the world.

The third race were half-human and half-animal. Their chief lived in Bower Cave on the old Coulterville Road in Yosemite Valley. The animal nature overcame the human half, and these people became our present animals and birds.

Skunk was chief of the fourth race who, like the third, were half-human and half-animal. Skunk was a bad chief. He ordered the hunters to bring him venison. He ate it all and gave the people -- including the hunters -- acorns and other common foods.

Skunk would place his hunters behind trees, and then he would let fly his horrible odor. The deer would run away from the smell toward the direction of the hidden hunters, who killed them with arrows.

The people wanted to kill Skunk. Badger dug a hole and the people filled it with red hot coals and then covered it over with soft earth. They asked Skunk to dance on that place, and as he danced the people praised him loudly. He danced on and on and finally sank into the hole. The people quickly covered him with large stones, but Skunk fought for his life. He shot his scent over and over, which caused the mountains to rise from the smooth surface of the earth.

The people rejoiced with a great feast of deer meat. Then they turned into the animals whose names they bore.

No one knows who the fifth race of people were, nor do they know their fate.

And then the earth was covered with water. Coyote told Frog he had decided to make people and various foods.

Frog thought it was not a good idea for people needed dry land upon which to live, and the entire world was water.

Coyote told Duck and Watersnake to dive under the water to see if they could find some dirt. They did not succeed.

Then Frog dived and returned with his hands full of sand. Coyote scattered this sand to make land for the people. He planted pine nuts, acorns and other food.

Coyote wanted to make some good people for the world. He made them with hands and feet like those of Lizard so that people could pick up food and shoot the bow and arrow.

Such were the beliefs of the Miwok. This is how modern historians tell of the development of the Miwok culture:

The ancestors of the Penutians wandered into central California around 2000 B.C. For 1500 years, or to 500 B.C., the peoples throughout the entire area of what is now the state of California had a relatively uniform and simple culture. They had not as yet developed the custom of marrying outside the basic groups of kinsmen. These groups were headed by chiefs, and culture rested on the means and methods of gathering food.

The second period (500 B.C. to 500 A.D.) saw northern and southern influences pinching in on the central part of California. The Penutians by now were firmly locked into the California heartlands.

From 500 A.D. to 1200 A.D. the localized cultures throughout the state became increasingly differentiated. The Kuksu religion was developed during this period in the central part of California.

The fourth period (1200 to 1800) saw the historic cultures of the various tribes perfected. In the California heartland, the Kuksu religion grew more elaborate, and the foot-drum was introduced.

Language root is the tool science uses to group the various aboriginal tribes of the Americas.

We have already seen how the white man has linked the Miwok with four of his cousin tribes (Wintun, Maidu, Costanoan and Yokuts) into the Penutian family. This group -- a ''compact and indissoluble unit'' -- held sway over the center of California.

The six other basic California Indian linguistic stocks were scattered over the remainder of the state and not always in contiguous units.

The Hokan were the most geographically diverse, spotted about California from the extreme north to the extreme south, including the Washo to the east of the Miwok, and the Indians along the coast south of Monterey.

14

Sam Casoose Domingo, Central Miwok, Tuolumne. (1923).

Tom Williams, Central Miwok. (1913).

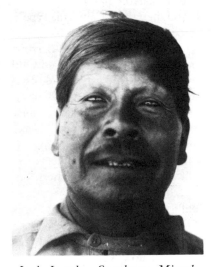

Mrs. Peedie Roan, Southern Miwok, Madera County.(1922).

Jack Lundy, Southern Miwok, Mariposa County. (1922).

The Algonkians, Athapascans, Yukians and Lutuamians held small territories in the northern part of the state.

The Shoshoneans were masters of the land east of the Sierra, the desert regions, and the Los Angeles basin.

So much for language type. What of cultural groupings? We find three

15

distinctive aboriginal civilizations in the state.

In the northwest corner of California were the southernmost tribes influenced by those remarkable Indians of the north Pacific Coast, with their extravagant potlatch mentality and fanatic competitive bent.

Southern California was the extension of the great Southwestern cultural area, which includes such diverse peoples as the Aztecs of Mexico; the Hopi, Papago and Pima of Arizona; and the Ute of Utah and Colorado.

Thus, the northern and southern Californians were frontier extensions of cultures whose wellsprings lay great distances away geographically. Only in the central area of California -- the Penutian Empire -- do we have a truly typical California civilization, that is a civilization comparatively untouched by strong outside influences. And in the heart of this heart stand the Miwok.

Modern scientists have still more interesting ways of dissecting the California aborigines, dividing them into the ''low faced'' and the ''high faced''.

The ''low faced'', called the ''Yuki type'', is split into two sub-groups, the ''broad-headed'' or ''California type'', and the ''narrow-headed, narrow-nosed'' or ''Western Mono type''.

And then the ''California type'' is split in three: the ''narrow-nosed'', ''broad-nosed'', and ''tall''.

Thus, the Miwok is a ''narrow-nosed, broad-headed low-face''. Or, if you prefer, a ''narrow-nosed California-type Yuki type''. So too are the Hupa, Modoc, Washo, Yokuts, Diegeunos, Cahuilla and others. (One often wonders as to the observer-scientist's head shape.)

Of all the living Indians subjected to the scientists' caliphers in the 1920's, the Southern Miwok was found to be the least variable as a group. That is, the cranial measurements -- length of nose, breadth of ears, etc. -- of the various Miwok subjects were the closest to being identical of any California tribe. The Northern Pomo were the most variable. Put another way, the Southern Miwok were the greatest look-alikes of any of the California tribes.

The ax and stone celt were unknown to the Miwok and the other California Indians. They used one stone driven by another to do the job. No matter how well this method might work, this practice provided these people with a handy label: ''stone-age men''.

The Miwok never ''advanced to the stage'' of making pottery, and thus earned another demerit from the white man. He wove beautiful and nearly perfect baskets that were watertight and could be used for cooking. Also, these vessels were much lighter than pottery and consequently more portable. No matter. The Miwok did not invent the scales used for measuring man. They are read by their inventors.

16

4

White Man

We know what happened to the Indians of California.

But, what happened to the white man?

What caused "civilized" men to turn barbarian?

Curiously enough, it took almost exactly a hundred years for the white man to accomplish his work of extermination in California.

Captain Pedro Fages and Fra Juan Crespi, standing near the junction of the Sacramento and San Joaquin Rivers in 1772, were the first white men to see the Sierra Nevada range. The year 1872 is generally regarded as the date Indian resistance came to an end in these mountains.

The Sierra Nevada chronology clearly shows that the Miwok's real troubles began with the gold rush. Prior to 1848, direct contact with the white men of the coast and valley was minimal.

1776 -- The Sierra Nevada name is noted by the Franciscan missionary, Pedro Font, as the Anza expedition moves northward through the valley on its way to colonize San Francisco.

1806 -- Ensign Gabriel Moraga leads an expedition to the lower reaches of the Merced River.

1826 -- Jedediah Smith crosses near Cajon Pass at the head of a party of trappers.

1833 -- Trappers, led by J. R. Walker, cross what is now part of Yosemite National Park.

1841 -- The Bartleson Party is the first group of immigrants to cross Sonora Pass.

1844 -- The first covered wagon is brought over the Sierra Nevada by the Townsend-Murphy party.

1847 -- J. B. Alvarado sells the "Mariposa Grant" to J. C. Fremont for $3000.

So far, so good for the native Californians. But then, in 1848, gold is discovered and the rush is on.

Within three years, Tuolumne and Mariposa Counties are organized; Joseph Screech discovers Hetch Hetchy Valley; the Indians attack J. D. Savage's Fresno River trading post which prompts organization of the Mariposa Battalion to "capture" the Indians of Yosemite.

There were an estimated 133,000 Indians in California in 1770; 15,850 in 1910. Between these two dates, the Penutians dropped from 57,000 to 3500; the Interior Miwok from 9000 to 700.

While the Spaniards, except as possible sources of epidemics, had little contact with the foothill and mountain Indians, they differed from the predominantly Anglo-Saxon gold seekers in some very important ways.

The Spaniards viewed the California Indians as a natural resource to be exploited -- to be Christianized and to be made into producers of commodities. The Church and the State were forces to be reckoned with in Spanish California.

Diego De Borica, seventh Spanish governor of California, appointed June 10, 1793, figured his most difficult political problem was the ever growing demand for land grants from his fellow countrymen. An incredible ''problem'' when one considers the vast amount of land California represents and the almost miniscule Spanish population of the day (in 1810, there were 2050 whites in Alta California, 17,150 mission Indians) -- plus the obvious need to add to that population to insure Spain's fragile hold on the Pacific slope.

De Borica was bothered because he was convinced the native Californians were the legitimate owners of California's soil. There were 13 missions in California at that time, stretching from San Diego to San Francisco. Each claimed its limits of jurisdiction extended at least half-way to the adjoining missions. Most of the land intervening between the missions was occupied by natives living in rancherias.

De Borica advised that land grants only be made in exceptional cases, and only in the vicinity of missions -- and only where ''no harm could come to the Indians' rights.''

There were growing instances of barbarous cruelty by Spaniards toward the Indians, especially along the frontiers. During one year in San Francisco, for instance, 203 Indians died from unnatural causes and 200 others ran away.

De Borica, the governor, used what power he had to fight for the rights of the natives -- and he was successful in bringing about some reforms.

The Spaniard was Mediterranean in his racial outlook. Intermarriage with indigenes, which created the mestizo, was regarded as a natural result of conquest.

The Anglo-Saxon's invasion presented some sharp contrasts in attitude. He came in a short space of time and in great numbers, more than 100,000 in the Mother Lode alone during the height of the gold rush. There were no formal church controls and no adequate state restraints.

The Anglo-Saxon was prone to regard anyone with a skin color different from his own as his mental and moral inferior. To marry a native was an

18

antisocial act, and the white partner could never regain his place under the white man's sun.

All non-Christian belief was regarded by the Anglo-Saxon as superstition.

The gold seekers were of two general classes: the moral, ethical and law-abiding; and the floaters, irregulars, failures, malcontents and contemptuous as well as the outright criminal. But both groups -- saints and sinners -- agreed that the natives had no rights -- certainly not to property and not even to life when the white man's most insignificant right was in conflict.

Theodora Kroeber wrote in *Ishi*, the biography of the last "wild" Indian who came in contact with the white world in 1911: "Many of us in California number among our ancestors a grandparent or a great-grandparent who came ... (to California) ... looking for a home. We have been taught to regard with pride the courage and ingenuity of these ancestors, their stubbornness in carving out a good life for their children. It is neither meet nor needful to withdraw such affectionate respect and admiration; it is perhaps well to remind ourselves that the best and gentlest of them did not question their right to appropriate land belonging

Gold mining scene showing Indian miners among the whites. Early gold-seekers exploited Indians, giving them trinkets in exchange for stream nuggets. Records of working Indians in back-breaking diggings as shown in this photo are rare: Indians were strangers to manual labor and regular work hours.

to someone else, if Indian -- the legal phrase was 'justifiable conquest'.''

The Anglo-American system simply had no meaning to the native Californian. If the latter could make the transition, he was granted an indifferent right to exist. But, if there was any conflict whatsoever with the system, the native was eliminated -- ruthlessly, either by a quick death from a bullet in the head; or by a slow death -- confinement in a reservation.

We get a clear picture of the displacement suffered by native Californians in the mid-19th Century from Lansford Hastings' *The Emigrants' Guide to Oregon and California,* published in 1845:

"The Indians of this country are not migratory, but it is seen, that they have, in numerous instances, abandoned their old haunts, and re-established in other portions of the country, but for what cause, it is difficult to ascertain, with any degree of certainty, for the sites which have been thus abandoned appear in many instances to possess advantages much superior to those which have been subsequently selected.

"As far as can be ascertained, the desolating ravages of war have been the chief causes of these repeated removals, for villages of fifty, or even a hundred of these huts, are frequently seen, which have the appearance of having been their ancient haunts, but which are now abandoned, the ground at and around which is covered with human skulls.

"Upon examining several of these huts, of these abandoned villages, I very readily found that whatever the cause of this mortality might have been, it was evidently inflicted upon them when within their huts...''

We do not have to guess at what the white man considered the best solution to the ''Indian Problem''. The library stacks are full of first-hand accounts of pioneer dealings with the tribesmen. But none is more to the point of this narrative than the Journal of William Perkins, a Canadian who reached the diggings in 1849.

Perkins was no uncouth roughneck plunderer. Nor was he blind to the moral implications of killing human beings who happened to be Indians. He eloquently questioned the morality of the act -- yet himself pulled the trigger of his rifle! ''Stern necessity of pioneer life!'' is the reason he gives. We cannot judge the validity of that reason from the vantage point of historic hindsight, for we are not pioneers in an unforgiving land. We must remember also that in battle -- and the gradual conquest of the American continent was a battle -- one does not distinguish between ''good'' enemies and ''bad'' enemies. The Indian was the enemy. The white-Indian wars dehumanized both combatting sides, but in truth the conquest of Miwok lands took place with such rapidity that the Miwok was beaten before he knew what hit him. In fact, in this fight the opening bell never rang. The Miwok's first stand and last stand were as one: they simply did not take place in the sense that an entire people united to meet the challenge of a conquerer. The Miwok was swallowed up village by village -- in one gulp.

20

Oak-bordered Woods Creek near Jamestown, south of Sonora, was site of gold discoveries in 1848 which brought a stampede of miners into the very heart of Miwok country. Ironically -- and, perhaps, symbolically -- Woods Creek at its Highway 49 crossing is today the site of a malodorous sewage treatment plant whose stench welcomes modern visitors to the Mother Lode.

The Perkins Journal is unique in the literature of the California Gold Rush, for unlike almost all other first-hand recorders of the '49er adventure who concentrated in their writings on the journey to California, Perkins begins his serious accounting after he arrives on the scene. And, too, he landed in the Southern Mines at a time when his fellow adventurers were flooding the Northern Mines. Add to this the fact he settled in Sonorian Camp, the California center of Mexican and Chilean miner concentration, and what Perkins has to tell us is doubly significant. Here we have a picture of white-Indian relations at the moment before the massive white influx that overruns the natives, and in an area of mixed white population containing elements that at least had a history of co-existence with the native Californians.

Perkins himself was an admirer of the Latin culture. So much so, in fact, that after he left Tuolumne County in 1852, he settled in Argentina where he rose to some importance as a colonization promoter.

On February 1, 1850, a small party of Miwoks raided a Sonora corral and drove off seven mules. A Mexican in charge of the animals was murdered. We can assume from the heart-of-winter date that the Indians were after food -- not sport or retaliation.

21

"This is temerity," wrote Perkins, "to be visited with swift vengeance, if we desire to sleep in security; so a call for volunteers was made at once, and there being three stout men in our establishment, we felt in honor bound to send one, and although a tramp up into the snowy mountains at this season of the year is not to be envied, with magnanimous loyalty, I volunteered. I put my blankets and a bag of provisions on a mule, provided myself with lots of ammunition and a 'Mississippi yager', stuck a heavy bowie knife in the leg of one of my boots, put a plug of cavendish in my pocket with a short pipe in the bosom of my thick red flannel shirt, and was ready for a start."

It may not be fair to conjecture Perkins' mood, but we can rule out a mood of extreme desperation, whereas the Indians who stole into Sonora after muleflesh may very well have been desperate.

"We were all on foot," wrote Perkins, "with three mules to carry the blankets and provisions, as we should be obliged to climb mountains, when any weight would necessarily impede our progress. We struck the trail of our Indian marauders about three miles from town; here we found it broad and well marked, and about twelve hours old. About ten miles further we came up with our Mexican friends who had passed through Sonora the day before. They had also struck the trail, some hours before us, but were too timid to follow it into the mountains. However, on seeing a company of eighteen well armed white men, they were inspired with a new and wonderful zeal, and followed us with a great show of courage."

The party camped at the Lewis ranch, and

"the next day we were off at daylight, and struck at once into the mountains; not into the passes, but following the trail step for step, through the most difficult route, the snow being in many places up to our knees.

"About twelve o'clock, ten of our Mexican companions gave up, and took the back track. We kept on and in a couple of hours came upon a deserted Indian rancho. The trail here crossed a mountain stream, swollen by the late heavy rains. How the savages had got the mules across this torrent is more than I can say. We were obliged to make a bridge. The mountains beyond this stream were very difficult to surmount, and the Indians seem to have taken the most inaccessible passages, in order to evade pursuit. It was tremendous work for Christians, but we trudged along bravely."

A second night's camp was made on the banks of the Stanislaus River, and

"the next morning we were again on the march by daylight, and were four hours climbing the mountain that bordered the river. Once on the top we found the trail running along the ridge, and as the Indians generally place their towns on the highest ridges, we surmised that the ranch belonging to the marauding party we were in pursuit of, could not be very distant. We therefore sent out our best men as scouts in order to discover the town and bring us word, so that we might take it by surprise.

"After a six hours march one of our scouts brought us the welcome intelligence that the town we were looking for was only half a mile distant. We halted and made the necessary preparations, and then marched on in the strictest silence.

"Suddenly on turning an abrupt angle of a huge pile of rocks, we came upon a large Rancheria, consisting of more than a hundred well built huts in the shape of beehives. In the center was the council house...about fifty feet in circumference. On the opposite side was a sloping hill at the foot of which ran a stream of water."

The theft of the mules, and the murder of the Mexican, are now to be avenged and the Indians taught a lesson.

"The alarm had been already given, and the hill was covered with men, women and children, the latter running like deer, while the men with their bows and arrows stood their ground; but the first volley of rifle bullets was too much for them. The affair did not last more than five minutes. I did not fire my rifle more than three times. We were too much fatigued to follow the agile rascals. Some of the most active of the scouts followed the enemy for two or three miles, and the reverberation of their rifle shots was heard now and then; some time after we were in quiet possession of the town.

"The tribes of Indians inhabiting these mountains are called Root-Diggers, and are the most wretched of all North American Indians. They are about four feet high, with very large heads and huge shocks of hair, coarse and black. Their limbs are very small; their legs are no larger than the arm of a moderate size man. Their feet are ridiculously small, and their hands and fingers long and exceedingly thin and slender. They go entirely naked even in the severe region in which they reside, and subsist on roots, acorns, berries and the small edible part of the pine cone, which is found in great abundance in all the mountains of California."

Perkins, of course, was not a scientist, and his observations reflect his opinions more than they report facts.

But he is able to distinguish between the native and transient Indians. "These Indians (the Miwok)," wrote Perkins, "are not the depredators on the white settlements; but they harbor, in large numbers, the 'Mission Indians' of the lower country, who are much more daring, and are physically rather a fine bodied race. They have been, and are, very prejudicial to the settlements, robbing mules and horses and even murdering the solitary miner. They carry their plunder to the almost inaccessible fastnesses of the Root-Diggers, with whom they share, receiving in return hospitality, and the course provisions of their allies."

It does not seem to occur to Perkins that all these Indians are fighting for -- all they want -- is to preserve their way of life and have enough food to live on.

Perkins continues:

"In our conflict with the Indians even in the heat of combat, we were anxious to avoid killing the Root-Diggers; aiming only at those Indians whom we noticed with dresses on, as the lower country Indian always wears some piece of clothing or finery, if it be only a red handkerchief round his head, or a colored calico shirt.

"I know that for my part, I was very much shocked and pained on seeing two or three bodies of these poor wretched Root-Diggers, who had probably been shot by the Mexicans, who are not scrupulous in the matter of bloodshed.

"The meat of the six mules was already hanging on the branches of the trees along with that of others stolen before. It is something strange that these Indians prefer mule flesh to any other, as the Pampa Indians of Buenos Aires prefer that of mares.''

Stranger still is the fact that a well-educated, intelligent 1849 white man could not guess that eating mule flesh was not a matter of choice over some other kind of meat (as if the Miwok had only to wander over to a butcher shop to make another selection); but a matter of life and death for a people living on high ground in February, with access blocked to lower elevations and their food resources.

After eating some mule flesh (Perkins preferred the hind leg of a dog, but drew no connotation from it), the party surveyed the spoils of victory.

''We found in the Rancheria a large quantity of stolen clothes,'' wrote Perkins, ''plenty of handsomely made baskets; immense quantities of acorns and pine cones (probably the bulk of the community's remaining winter stores), with bread made from the pounded flour of the two latter. This bread we tried to eat, but found it exceedingly disgusting to the palate; bitter, and with a flavor that was nauseous in the extreme.

''Collecting every thing moveable, we piled all in the ranches, and set fire to the whole town, in imitation of the warriors of the middle ages.''

Middle ages, indeed! A barbarous act, condemning women and children to suffering and death by exposure and starvation. Condemning the men to a hard choice: starve and watch your kin starve, or raid the white men for food and thus escalate the conflict with the well-armed and invincible invaders.

Of course, Perkins is not resting easy over the fate of the Indian village:

''After the excitement of the fray had subsided, I could not help asking myself the question, as to how far we were warranted in destroying life and property to such an extent; for although the value of property destroyed probably did not amount to much, still it was the whole amount of worldly goods possessed by the tribe. The houses, we may readily believe, have as great a value, comparatively speaking, to their owners, as ours in Sonora. Their baskets, and above all their supply of provisions, may certainly be placed on a par with our household goods. And we had invaded and destroyed the lives and property of these poor, miserable people, to chastise what in their eyes is no crime.

''To say the truth, I was not entirely satisfied with myself. For the loss of life amongst the Mission Indians I did not feel much compunction; for they are a bad set, and the indisputable law of self-preservation, if not entirely a satisfactory warrant, suffices at all events, to pacify the conscience. But in this case, not only did Root-Diggers fall in the conflict, but the women and children suffered from the loss of their homes and necessaries of life.

''Stern necessity of pioneer life! We invade a land that is not our own, we arrogate a right through pretense of superior intelligence and the wants of civilization, and if the aborigines dispute our title, we destroy them!''

Despite this refreshing soul-searching, the next morning Perkins and his companions burned another large Rancheria!

''We now turned towards home,'' continued Perkins, ''and on the way came across another Rancheria, deserted by its owners. This we also burnt.''

After returning to Sonora, Perkins reported ''another party of Americans which started up the mountains after us, in pursuit of Indians who had murdered a miner, had just returned with a pair of scalps. I think that Sonora will be free from their depredations in future.''

On the 20th of February, Perkins noted: ''Two men came in today with the intelligence that, of a party of five, all Texans, attacked in the mountains by the Indians, they only escaped. They left their companions dead, and are themselves badly wounded. Here then is the commencement of a warfare that seems, from past history, to be inevitable in every country where the Caucasian race comes in contact with the aborigines of the soil. The result will also be inevitable -- the total destruction of the native races.''

Perkins' entry for August 7, 1850, is revealing:

''Last night a poor Indian lost his life through an ill-timed and cruel jest. A party of young men, rather the worse for liquor, seeing the Indian intoxicated, commenced amusing themselves at his expense. One of the party, remarking that the Indian had a sinister looking face, offered to wager that he could be induced to commit a crime. The bet was taken, and the young man put a pistol, unloaded in the Indian's hand, and told him to go and rob a man whom he pointed out walking up the street.

''The Indian, taking the pistol, marched at once up to the man and presenting it said: 'Deme su dinero, o le matare. Give me your money or I will kill you!'

''He had hardly time to finish the sentence, when the man addressed pulled out his pistol and shot the poor devil down. The young man who had incited the Indian to commit the assault, was arrested; but it turned out that he had, for the last four or five days, been actually a maniac, from the effects of liquor himself.''

January 12, 1851:

''The Indians are becoming more mischievous than ever. A party of five men has just been attacked by them, a few miles from Sonora, and all the five are badly wounded with arrows. A body of hunters immediately started in pursuit, and, overtaking the savages the same day, a smart fight ensued, the result of which was a booty of twenty Indian scalps. The rest escaped up the mountains.

''What surprises me is, that the Indians have not attempted to fire the town at night. It might be done with the greatest ease and impunity, for there is never any guard; policemen, watchmen or sentinels are not known here, and the town, within a day's journey of a dozen, probably a score of Indian Rancherias full of our mortal enemies. Really, we are superbly careless of our lives in this paradoxical country.''

Finally, on March 6, 1852, Perkins was able to write:

''...there seems to be a great change come over the savage tribes within the last twelve months. Last year it was almost impossible to keep mules in safety anywhere outside the town. Almost every night the Indians were prowling about and driving off cattle. Now we scarcely ever hear of the robbery of a mule. The aborigines have received so many severe chastisements, that they are moving farther up into the fastnesses of the Sierra Nevada, and seldom venture down. Like the deer they are

*An early engraving of a '49er lean-to. Miners were "forced
to live like Indians" in the Sierra Nevada foothills.*

retiring before the tread of the white man.

"What will they do when the tide of population advancing from the shores of the
Pacific meets the flood of immigration from the Atlantic side and hems them in on
the snowy ridge of the Cordilleras? 'The poor Indian!' His course is almost run on
this vast continent once so exclusively his own."

Let us turn now to a pioneer who can provide us with a more complete
answer to the question asked at the start of this chapter: What happened to
the white man? What happened to people, some of whom of high principle
in whose blood flowed the best of centuries of Western civilization? What
caused these people to treat the Indians, in Mrs. Kroeber's words, "with
such ferocious inhumanity and brutality?"

J. Goldsborough Bruff spent the winter of 1849-50 on the emigrant trail
leading south from Oregon, forced by illness to camp 32 miles short of his
goal.

For five months he ministered to the needs of the emigrants. He fed
them, warmed them, cheered them, let them sleep in his bed, and even
helped bury their dead -- and not one of them offered to take him the 32
miles to the rancho he sought!

"Many I recognized as old acquaintances as far back as Pittsburgh,"
wrote Bruff. "Large companies (they were then), with fine animals, a
great amount of provisions and stores, and smiling faces; now scattered,
broken, selfish stragglers, thin with hunger (and) anxiety."

26

The overland emigrants were dehumanized and brutalized by the incredible trek across a continent. Besides the filth and exertion and disease associated with the journey, they had been threatened and often killed by fearless, well-mounted and well-armed Plains and Great Basin Indians.

Too bad for the docile California Indian. He too could only be considered a good Indian when he was a dead Indian.

The name of Botellas, a Mother Lode mining camp, was changed to Jackson in 1850 to honor its most illustrious settler, Col. Alden Jackson. Why illustrious? Because he was a famous Indian fighter!

Killing an Indian and killing a rattlesnake were regarded as equally necessary acts -- something to talk about for a day or so. There was one old Butte County prospector, according to anthropologist T. T. Waterman, who had on his bed a blanket lined with Indian scalps. ''No reckoning was at any time demanded of him,'' Waterman wrote.

Bullets provide only one kind of death. Consider the kind of death Enos Christman, pioneer Sonora editor, describes in a letter written near Mariposa on March 21, 1850: ''This evening we were visited by a strolling band of Indians, six in number, armed with their bows and arrows and some of them almost nude, having nothing but a check shirt and cap on. They are a poor miserable-looking set of devils, speak a very little Spanish, and were out on a begging excursion. One of our neighbors gave them beef enough for supper and breakfast.''

Between 1850 and 1855, the California State Legislature passed three laws which legalized the termination of the native Californians.

The first law denied the natives the right to testify in court.

The second decreed that any white citizen could hail a native into court and have him declared a vagrant. The native could then be put up at auction and sold as a laborer to the highest bidder. The period of peonage was for four months and the only compensation to which the Indian was legally entitled was his keep.

The third law decreed that any native adult or child could be bound over to a white citizen. The proper name for this arrangement is slavery, but this term was avoided, for California was a free soil state.

The Federal Government was active, too, in settling matters with the California Indians. Following the gold rush, treaties with the leaders of 139 native bands were negotiated. In general these arrangements can be summed up as trades: the Indians gave to the white man what the white man wanted in exchange for what the white man didn't want.

Still, the official slate is not entirely unfavorable to the Indian. Thirteen of California's counties bear Indian names: Colusa, Inyo, Marin, Modoc, Mono, Napa, Shasta, Siskiyou, Sonoma, Tehama, Tuolumne, Yolo and Yuba.

5

First Impressions Are
Lasting Impressions

When historian Hubert H. Bancroft explained the reason for a particular California Indian habit or custom or condition of existence, he paid
very little attention to fact.

Unfortunately, from the 1880's to almost the present, what we have by
way of ''fact'' regarding the native Californians is pretty much what
Bancroft set down on paper.

Bancroft, however, judged the natives' culture by his own standards.
He made no effort to understand or appreciate what he saw, or to question
why the native Californians reacted to objects in their environment in a
manner different from the way the white man reacted to these same objects. He ignores the fact that these people had lived in peace and plenty for
centuries and fails to recognize the fact that, when he met the natives (if
indeed he ever did!), they had already lived for many years under the white
man's ruthless subjugation. Still, Bancroft took it upon himself to report
what he saw, or thought he saw, as fact, and to explain and interpret it in
terms of his own opinions, prejudices, and cultural values.

To be sure, anthropologist A. L. Kroeber has set the record straight,
even as have some popular writers on a national scale such as Helen Hunt
Jackson whose book, *A Century of Dishonor,* saved the Indian from
absolute extinction (and, paradoxically, so popularized pastoral Southern
California that the book is held chiefly responsible for the great population
influxes of 1890-1910 which wiped out pastoral Southern California and
any chance Indians in that part of the state ever had of returning to at least
a vestige of their old ways of life).

Why did California Indian women have an easy time of childbirth (if
indeed they did)? Bancroft knew: the ''sexes have their regular season for
copulation, just as animals have theirs.''

Did the California Indians play games? Wrote Bancroft: ''...though
naturally the very incarnation of sloth, at least as far as useful labor is
concerned, they have one or two games which require some exertion.''

What of hunting? Bancroft: ''The bestial laziness of the Central
Californian prevents him from following the chase to any extent, or from
even inventing efficient game-traps.''

What of their diet? Bancroft : "Reptiles and insects of all descriptions are greedily devoured; in fact, any life-sustaining substance which can be procured with little trouble, is food for them."

Also: "It is a well established fact that California Indians, even when reared by Americans from infancy, if they have been permitted to associate with others of their race, will, in the season of lush, blossoming clover, go out and eat it in preference to all other foods."

What of their personal habits? "...they are filthy in the extreme. Both their dwellings and their persons abound in vermin, which they catch and eat..."

And to summarize: "It is not until we reach the golden mean in Central California that we find whole tribes subsisting on roots, herbs and insects; having no boats, no clothing, no laws, no god; yielding submissively to the first touch of the invader; held in awe by a few priests and soldiers."

Even before the Spaniards had much contact with the Indians of Alta California, our concept of the Pacific Coast aborigines was pretty well formed -- Montalvo and his Amazons notwithstanding.

Even the Alsatian Jakob Baegert, generally regarded as one of the most sympathetic of the Jesuit priests toward the Baja California Indians whom they were converting, weighed the natives on European scales: "In general it can be said about the Californian that they are stupid, dull, coarse, dirty, insolent, ungrateful liars, lazy, slothful in the extreme, great gabbers, and in their intelligence and actions children to their dying day...in everything they follow their natural instincts after the manner of the brute beasts."

By 1897, Theodore H. Hittell (*History of California*) was able to tie the Alta California Indians to their Baja California neighbors without equivocation: "On account of their low grade in the scale of humanity, being with few exceptions as low as their neighbors in Lower California and therefore almost as degraded as any human beings on the face of the earth, they can hardly be described as divided into distinct tribes, but rather as one people varying only according to the regions they inhabited and the kinds of food upon which they lived."

Hittell, so typical of the turn-of-the-century history writer, digs deep in his garbage pail of adjectives and clearly reveals the basic weakness of scientific observation at least to that time: the native Californians were compared to other Indians who had certain characteristics which the white man, because of his own characteristics, respected.

"All were equally stupid and brutish," wrote Hittell. "In general they resembled mere omnivorous animals without government or law...they were a very different race from the Red Men on the Eastern side of the continent and can hardly be considered in any respect of the same blood."

29

"...there were amongst them few or no specimens of physical beauty..."

"...all accounts agree...the (California) Indians (were) among the most stupid, brutish, filthy, lazy and improvident of the aborigines of America..."

"...their stupidity was the result...of mental torpidity caused by idleness..."

It takes a writer of Bayard Taylor's sensitivity and humanness to wash the taste of a Hittell from the reader's mouth.

Taylor was one of the greatest travel writers of all time. He is as current today as he was in 1849 when he wrote *Eldorado,* the account of his visit to California.

Taylor does not tell us much directly about the Central California natives because he seldom engages in hearsay. He does tell us a great deal about the people who overran the Indians, and what they thought about their victims.

Taylor is caught in a rainstorm at a ranch on the "Cosumne River." This is Miwok country: "...I went into the house inhabited by the family and asked permission to dry myself at the fire. The occupants were two women, apparently sisters, of the ages of 18 and 30...They made no answer to my request, so I took a chair and sat down near the blaze. Two female tongues, however, cannot long keep silent, and presently the elder launched into a violent anathema against all emigrants, as she call them..."

They accused the almost destitute emigrants of stealing their supplies, and more:

"...most especially did the elder express her resentment against the said emigrants, on account of their treatment of the Indians. I felt disposed at first to agree with her wholly in their condemnation, but it appeared that she was influenced by other motives than those of humanity.

" 'Afore these here emigrants come,' said she, 'the Injuns were as well-behaved and bidable as could be; I liked 'em more 'n the whites. When we begun to find gold...we could get 'em to work for us day in and day out, fur next to nothin'. We told 'em the gold was stuff to whitewash houses with, and give 'em a hankercher for a tin-cup full; but after the emigrants begun to come along and put all sorts of notions into their heads, there was no gettin' them to do nothin'.' "

Objective observation is rare, because the Bayard Taylors are rare.

J. M. Hutchings attempted to explain the Miwok-white conflict in his book *In the Heart of the Sierras,* published in 1888.

At first, he reported all was well between Miwok and the first few prospectors. But, as more miners, more suppliers, more of the white man's goods and livestock made their appearance, trouble began.

The white man's tools, supplies and animals, according to Hutchings, "presented visible evidences of accumulating prosperity and wealth among the whites, that were unshared by the Indian. This soon bore the poisonous fruit of jealousy."

This led, according to Hutchings, to resentment, and finally, hatred of whites and "cupidity for their possessions began."

Jealousy and cupidity! As if the Indians had been denied nothing more than some bits of merchandise instead of their lands, their acorn-bearing trees, their game, their streams, their women, their peace, their right of movement, and their very lives.

"It is a well-known fact," reported Brig. Gen. Thomas B. Eastland to the governor of California in 1850, "that among our white population there are men who boast of the number of the Indians they have killed, and that not one shall escape."

What chance did the Miwok have against the mentality of a Major R. C. Barry, an early-day justice of the peace in Sonora?

Barry was "fearless and daring...considered one of the boldest and hardiest Texan Scouts. Reared in semi-savage country, he had but few opportunities for education. He could read and write after a fashion, but what he lacked in book-learning was amply compensated for by his indomitable will."

Barry was positive in everything. He brooked no contradiction to his decrees. As a Texan (actually, he had been born in Ireland in 1806), Barry had "an innate hatred of all Mexicans, which even extended to all foreigners who were not naturalized citizens."

This would, of course, place the Indian in an unenviable position before the Sonora bar of justice.

Here, in Barry's vernacular, is "civilization's" antidote for the Indian's "savagery":

"Caze No. 736. In this caze injun Bill was indited fur arsonizing a remada belonging to one John Brown by which he had lost all his furniture, bedding, tools, rifle, shotgun, pistol & c. Sentenced injun Bill to pay 32 dolars and pay for the remada and contents, in defalt to be comited to gaol 60 days and be flogged 3 times on his bear back. Costs of coort 32 dolars all of which was pade by some one. R. C. Barry, Justice Peace. Sonora City. October 7, 1851. U. H. Brown, Constable."

Col. Barry no doubt was no better or worse than the average white citizen of the Mother Lode at that time -- but the consequences to the natives of such a man controlling the mechanism of justice was staggering. California's so-called Indian peonage laws of the early 1850's were executed locally by Col. Barry and his fellow justices of the peace. To the native Californians, the rural justice was the sole arbitrator of his person and property. The California Indian had no status with the Federal government, and but an indifferent one with the state. The latter's legislators represented the very people who were so callously robbing the

Eight wood engravings and text for a special Hutchings California Magazine feature on the peculiar habits of the California Indians -- all lumped under the tribal designation "Digger". These cuts first appeared in 1856 and 1857.

HUTCHING'S CALIFORNIA SCENES.

THE CALIFORNIA INDIANS.

CATCHING GRASSHOPPERS.

GATHERING ACORNS.

AN INDIAN FANDANGO.

The California Indians are in stature short, but they are well and stoutly formed. Their features are coarse, broad, and of a dark chocolate color; their hair is black, heavy and matted. In their habits they are unclean, and indolent. Their huts are built of boughs, bark or old canvass, and are smoky, small and dirty. The women do the work, the men the eating, grumbling and sleeping. Their dress consists of any old and cast-off garments of the whites. Their food is acorns, roots, grasshoppers, wood and flower seeds, grass, clover, wild greens, rabbits, rats, squirrels and fish; but they prefer beef, biscuit and whiskey. The following are their methods of providing for their wants:—

GATHERING ACORNS.—A large cone-shaped basket is carried on the backs of the females fastened by a band running across their foreheads. The acorns, picked from beneath a tree, are thrown over their shoulders into the basket; they are then dried and stoned, or ground.

DIGGING ROOTS.—This is accomplished by the females and children Irving a pointed stick into the ground, and prying out the roots.

GATHERING SEEDS.—This is done by the females beating them with a bush into a cone-shaped basket.

CATCHING GRASSHOPPERS.—A hole is first dug

begins a monotonous "*feau, feau,*" with a reed whistle and wooden castanets—while the dancers keep time by a perpetual "*hi huh! hi huh*," until out of breath when they seat themselves to hear from the lips of their greatest chief, or patriarch the heroic deeds of their warrior ancestor; after which comes the feast That being over the dancing is renewed, and generally continued until morning, when they finish the remaining eatables and retire to rest under a large tree.

BURNING THE DEAD.—The motive which impels the California Indians to burn their dead, arises from their religious views. They believe in a vast and pleasant camping ground somewhere westward, where Indians live together in perpetual ease and plenty, and which is presided over by a great spirit of unspeakable goodness. They believe also in an evil spirit, who is constantly watching every opportunity to injure them, and who having the power to keep them out of heaven, it is their duty, by conciliation or stratagem, to thwart. They believe, also that the *heart* is immortal; that while the body is burning the heart leaps out, and if by noises or motions they can attract the evil spirit's attention the heart escapes to its heaven of rest and is forever safe; but if the body is buried, the evil one keeps continual guard over the grave, and when the heart would escape, it is made

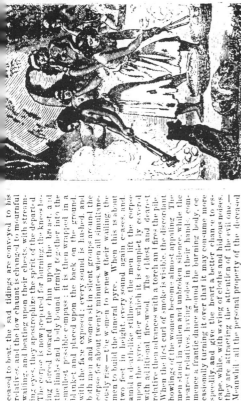

COOKING FOOD.

GRINDING ACORNS, &c.

Excelsior Print.

GRINDING ACORNS, &c.—Acorns, berries and flower seed are reduced to flour, and grasshoppers to paste, by the females pounding them upon a rock with an oblong stone, weighing from six to ten pounds.

COOKING FOOD.—Bowl-shaped and water-tight baskets, holding from two to four pecks, are filled with water, into which flour or meal is stirred; hot rocks are then put into the basket, until the water boils. It is then poured into smaller baskets to cool, when it is about the consistency of paste or mush, and is eaten from the baskets with the fingers. Rabbits, rats, squirrels, &c. are boiled until they are cooked. Grasshoppers are gathered into sacks and saturated with salt water; they are then placed in a hot trench and covered with hot rocks for about fifteen minutes, when they are eaten like shrimps; or, after being ground, are mixed with the soup or mush.

FANDANGOES.—These are popular and social gatherings of Indians for dancing, eating, laughing, talking, and learning the traditionary greatness of their nobly dead. Any particular tribe, wishing to give a fandango, send messengers to the chiefs of the surrounding tribes, who receive a small bundle of reeds or sticks, which show the number of days before it takes place. Preparations immediately commence upon an extensive scale, by those invited as well as those giving the invitation. Rabbits are snared, grasshoppers and fish are caught; acorns, roots, wild and flower seeds, clover, grass, wild greens and onions are provided in suitable quantities. As each Indian dresses according to his own extravagant notions of paint and feathers, several weeks are sometimes consumed in making head dresses of different colored feathers, nose and ear ornaments, and coat decorations, in every intricate variety of style and color. When the day arrives, groups of Indians may be seen wending their way toward the festive scene. In the evening, when all are assembled, the grand

ceased to beat, the sad tidings are conveyed to his relatives, and the low chaunt is changed to mournful wailing, and beating upon their chests, with streaming eyes, they apostrophize the spirit of the departed. The corpse is now prepared for burning, the deceased being forced toward the chin upon the breast, and the limbs and body bound firmly together into the smallest possible compass; it is then wrapped in a blanket and placed upon the back on the ground, with the face exposed; every sound is hushed, and both men and women sit in silent groups around the corpse for about twenty minutes, when all simultaneously rise—the women to renew their wailing, the men to build the funeral pyre. When this is about two feet in height, every sound again ceases, and amid a death-like stillness, the men lift the corpse upon the pyre, after which it is completely covered with additional fire-wood. The oldest and dearest relative then advances with a torch and fires the pile. When the first curl of smoke is visible, the discordant howlings of the women become almost appalling. The men stand in sullen and unbroken silence, while the nearest relatives, having poles in their hands, commence a frantic dance around the burning body, occasionally turning it over that it may consume more speedily, and give the heart a better chance to escape, while, with waving of cloths and hideous noises, they are attracting the attention of the evil one. Meanwhile all the personal property of the deceased is cast into the fire, his relatives frequently adding their own valuables, even to the scanty garments upon their persons, that he may want nothing in the great camping ground. When the whole is consumed, the ashes are scraped together, and a rude wreath of flowers, weeds and brush is placed around them. A portion of the ashes being mixed with some pitch, is spread over the faces of the relatives, as a badge of mourning, which is allowed to remain till it wears off, which is generally about six months.

BURNING THEIR DEAD.

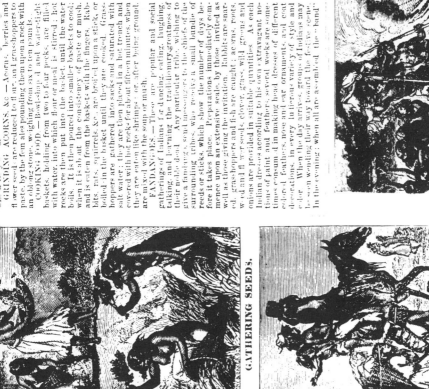

GATHERING SEEDS.

MODE OF TRAVELING.

natives of their lands. It would have been a political miracle for the California legislature in gold rush times even to recognize the most insignificant Indian "right".

And thus it was that when the Col. Barry's were administering justice, the Indian was a non-person. There was no power above the justice of the peace to which the Indian could appeal his case, even if someone had been around who was friendly to the Indian cause and who would have taken the time to explain the intricate mechanics of appeal.

Can the great naturalist John Muir balance Col. Barry?

Not really. Read between the lines:

"Even the young Digger Indians have sufficient love for the brightest of (the flowers) found growing in the mountains to gather them and braid them as decorations for the hair...

"And I was glad to discover, through the few Indians that could be induced to talk on the subject, that they have names for the wild rose and the lily, and other conspicuous flowers, whether available for food or otherwise..."

How did the popular press describe the Sierra Nevada Indians? By scanning an article in *Hutchings' California Magazine* for April, 1859, we come across a wide range of reporting that can hardly be characterized as objective:

"With all their failings, it cannot be denied that the California Indians are an interesting people...

"As these Indians are simply men and women, and without doubt the lowest in morality and intellectual ability on this continent..."

And

"...we wish to give our testimony in favor of the Reservations established by government to teach the Indian race the arts of agriculture, and the principles of self reliance (!). They are doing much to ameliorate the condition of the race, and in staying the sweeping hand of annihilation. But while we accord this much to the system, we enter our protest to the promiscuous and libidinous intercourse allowed at these reservations by those placed in charge. In our opinion, founded upon observation, no officer should be appointed, no white man employed who has not a wife to accompany him there; and who could have as elevating an influence with the females as the husband has with the males.

"We would also suggest the desirability of teaching the mechanic arts, in all its various branches, to the men; and of giving some suitable and acceptable employment to the women. Active employment being as great a civilizer among men as any code of morals ever promulgated."

Whatever else we can call it, we cannot call the white man's predominant attitude toward the Miwok as being one of compassion.

As late as 1959 we could read (in Irene Paden and Margaret Schlichtmann's *The Big Oak Flat Road to Yosemite*) so untempered a passage as this: "There were a few skirmishes between the miners and the Indians who either lived on the spot or came in season to gather

HUTCHINGS'
CALIFORNIA MAGAZINE.

VOL. III.   APRIL, 1859.   No. 10.

SCENES AMONG THE INDIANS OF CALIFORNIA.

The cover of Hutchings California Magazine *for April, 1859, featured a trio of "Digger Indians" -- presumably a bead- and basket-bearing suitor at right, a contemplative father, and a not-reluctant daughter. Hutchings, who went on to pioneer the Yosemite Valley tourist business after his magazine folded, made a swing through the gold country for the material that went into his highly subjective articles.*

acorns, evidenced by a large stationary mortar rock with many griding holes north of the road at the entrance to the town (Big Oak Flat). The affairs, in which a few arrows and pistol shots were let loose happily and at random, resulted in little but a pleasurable relief from monotony as far as the white men were concerned.''

Ten years later, in 1969, author John Greenway in *Folklore of the Great West,* offered this gem: ''Adult Indians played, too, whenever they grew weary of raping, looting and killing.''

The American Indian Historical Society, with headquarters in San Francisco, recently issued a publication, *Textbooks and the American Indian,* which is devastatingly critical of the Indian fare being presented in our schools. It is as if we had learned nothing about the nature of man since Bancroft's time.

Some examples:

From the California state adopted textbook, *California's Own History,* this passage is cited: ''They (the California Indians) also enjoyed some things we would not think of eating. They smacked their lips over fat worms and toasted grasshoppers.''

Comment: ''This is facetious provincialism. The worms and roasted grasshoppers have been food for many other people besides the Indians, for many thousands of years. The connotation is that of a 'strange' people, not like other human beings...The gold rush in California is treated from the white man's point of view. Indians were mere impediments on the rush to the mines. As this author explains on page 168, the miners had a hard time getting to the mines: 'Then came a hard climb to the Pit River, past dangerous Indians'.''

The fourth grade public school text, *California and the West,* brought forth this comment: ''General failure to understand Indian culture is shown in this textbook...on page 22 we learn that 'in return for gifts, the Indians showed the newcomers where to find water.' This insidious insult against the native people is an indication of the rest of the book...''

The public school text, *California, A History,* contains this passage: ''...the Indians had better food and clothing (in the missions) than they had ever had. They were more comfortable than they had ever been.'' Comment: ''Such propaganda is actually an insult to the intelligence...the statement referring to ''wild Indians'' on page 126 is a gross insult...so much of the information given in this book is inaccurate, distorted, and unsubstantiated, that the book may be judged as absolutely unacceptable...In dealing with the gold rush...there is no mention of Indian sufferings, rape and genocide, etc., which also exist in the record of documented evidence. The author writes as though the Indians were dead, for on page 277, it is stated: 'Some of these (new) laws would seem very surprising to the Indians and the early Californians'.''

Regarding *Stories California Indians Told,* a state-adopted elementary school text, the Indian Historical Society publication commented: "Coyote stories are told largely for adult sophisticated entertainment...nevertheless, this author chooses to utilize them for the pleasure of the children. This is a common error. While such behavior among the white person who chooses to write about Indians amuses us, we are not amused by the author's dedication: 'For all boys and girls who like Indians and animals'."

And from the fourth grade supplementary book for public school use, *California Gold Days:* "The gold miners are glorified beyond all evidence to the contrary as to their character, reasons for coming, and way of life. On page 92, 'It was surprising that there was not more trouble. The miners were men of all kinds. All had to work together. A hundred thousand people in the wild, rough life of the gold mines! Whoever they were, every man had an equal chance. All had to play fair and follow the rules. This was a true democracy.' If democracy was really represented by the hanging committees, the vigilantes, the kangaroo courts, and the killing of a man without trial, then democracy is not understood by this writer. If justice and democracy mean the attempted genocide and extermination of a whole race of people, because they stood in the way of gold, then this type of democracy is not for human beings. There is not one word of criticism of the gold miners. The Indians are mentioned only inadvertently. There is no explanation of Native conditions, land stealing, their way of life, and their intense suffering under the rule of the Great God Gold. No understanding is possible, as a result of this book, about the condition of the country during the days of the gold rush. The descriptions of how gold is mined, how great and adventurous it is, can only send the young student into a mercenary dream world. The book as a whole is unrealistic, inaccurate, and a chamber of commerce tract to glorify the gold miners."

The white man is loathe to put down his scales. The Sierra Nevada Indians of the 1850's were drawn into the U.S.-Soviet idealogical struggle in a book published in 1949.

The Lakeside Press (R. R. Donnelley & Sons, Chicago) published *Pictures of the Gold Rush California* in that year. The book includes a selection on "The Indians" from Alonzo Delano's *Life on the Plains and the Diggings,* first published in 1853.

Delano settled on the Feather River north of Miwok country. Regarding the Indians, he wrote: "...all seemed affectionate and kind to each other, and readily shared a tid-bit. When laying out my plot, I employed a young Indian to carry stakes. At dinner I gave him an ample plateful, when two other Indians came along and sat down without ceremony and shared his meal as readily as if it had been their own. For the purpose of trying two boys who came into my store, I would give one of them a single cracker, when he would invariably break it in two and give half to his companion...''

Milo Milton Quaife, the ''scholarly editor'' of the Lakeside Classics, offered this footnote comment on the sharing habits of Delano's Indian friends -- and again bear in mind, Dr. Quaife is writing in 1949: ''This conduct (of the Indians) had a significance which seems to have escaped our author (Delano). The primitive North American Indian was pretty much of a communist with respect to material goods. As a consequence, there was practically no inducement for the individual warrior to labor, since those who did not would join in consuming the fruit of his toil. With such a social concept, but little in the way of progress could ever be achieved.''

Quaife does not appreciate the generosity and sense of brotherhood inherent in the natives' behavior but instead criticizes what he sees as a lack of individual initiative.

In a modern high school text *(The Golden State)* we still get strong echoes of Bancroft. Despite the advantages of climate and the abundance of wild plant and animal food, report the authors, ''the first inhabitants of California made little progress toward developing a civilized way of life.''

The authors marvel at the Indians' ability to learn mechanical arts ''as illustrated in the remains of California missions, erected almost entirely by Indian workmen under the direction of friars.''

And under the same direction and apparently to their everlasting credit, the California Indians learned how to be ''skillful carpenters, weavers, farmers and cattle herders.''

The art of living in harmony with nature for unnumbered centuries is not, alas, to be regarded as a skill.

6

The Miwok's Self—The World Is Two

The Sierra Nevada's summers are hot and dry, its winters cold and wet. The Miwok's life was tied to the rhythm of these seasons.

And if the earth is half heat and half cold, half water and half land, half dry and half wet, half male and half female, half sky and half earth, half young and half old, half light and half dark; so too must the dwellers of that earth -- the people -- be of two families.

Thus the Miwok by some unknown formula divided themselves into balanced halves -- totemic moieties -- the land people and the water people.

The father's moiety determined that of his children, both male and female. It was taboo to marry a person from the same moiety, but this was not a rigidly enforced restriction. The Miwok themselves say that even before the coming of the white man, a marriage within a moiety evoked protest, but no attempt was made at actual interference. In modern times it was estimated one marriage in four violated the moiety taboo, accounted for in part by the fact -- again unexplained -- that the land side had an estimated twenty percent more members than did the water side.

When choosing teams for a game, in some cases it was water people versus land people. Or, at a funeral or mourning anniversary, custom dictated that people of the opposite moiety had a formal assistance role to fulfill.

In marriage, the ideal, most correct, most natural Miwok union was between certain relatives of the opposite moiety. The only explanation for this can be summed up in one word: tradition.

Some Miwok men -- if they could afford it -- had more than one wife. There is no evidence that sex was anything other than normal for the Miwok. That is, there was no more or no less pre-marital sex, adultery or even incest among the Miwok than there was among other people in other times. Sex is sex, and the Miwok was human. We do not find a celebration of sex in his folklore. In a word, his sex life was very, very normal.

A Miwok man could not marry his sister's daughter; father's sister's daughter; daughter-in-law; brother's son's wife; son's wife's sister; mother's older sister; father's brother's wife; or mother's earlier co-wife.

Of a man's female relatives of the opposite moiety, he could marry: his dead brother's wife; his dead wife's sister; his wife's brother's daughter; his wife's father's sister. He also could marry any of these three females in a polygymous union during his wife's lifetime.

The Miwok man sometimes married his first cousin -- but only his mother's brother's daughter -- that is, his cross-cousin.

In some Miwok localities, so close a marriage was frowned upon. A second cousin or some other distant relative of the opposite moiety was regarded as proper.

In theory, a man bought his bride -- but in practice the prospective son-in-law would "pay" for his bride with a deerskin -- or by helping the family for a period of time. However, formal bargaining or haggling was not practiced. The payment was actually a token.

The Miwok's speech taboos guaranteed much domestic tranquility. This very formalized system stems, perhaps, from the smallness of the communal unit -- averaging about one hundred persons. A Miwok lived all the days of his life within the confines of this narrow circle.

The Miwok man did not communicate directly with his brothers; nor did the Miwok woman speak with her sisters. Further, the Miwok man did not speak to his mother-in-law or her sisters, and the Miwok woman did not speak to her father-in-law or his brothers. There were still other speech taboos among relatives depending on moiety considerations.

When speech was absolutely necessary in the taboo situations described above, and there was no third person present to act as go-between, communication was carried on in the plural tense. That is, the speakers acted as if there were more than two people present.

And as the earth and its people were divided into land and water, so too was every other thing in creation -- plant and animal -- so divided.

The land-side was made up of these totems: bear, puma, wildcat, dog, fox, raccoon, tree squirrel, badger, jack rabbit;

Eagle, condor, raven, magpie, hawk, chicken hawk, great owl, blue jay, woodpecker, yellow-hammer, goldfinch;

Creeper, lizard, yellow-jacket, katydid;

Sugar pine, black oak, pine nuts, manzanita, tobacco, tule, salmon-berry;

Sky, sun, stars, night, fire, earth, salt;

Bow, arrows, quiver, drum, ear plug, and feather headdress.

The water-side consisted of:

Deer, antelope, coyote, beaver, otter, buzzard;

Falcon, burrowing owl, meadowlark, killdeer, hummingbird, kingbird, bluebird, dove, quail, goose, swan, crane, jacksnipe, kingfisher;

Frog, salamander, water snake, turtle, salmon, ant, bee, caterpillar, cocoon, butterfly, snail, haliotis;

Jimson weed, white oak, vetch, oak gall, wild cabbage;

Cloud, rain, fog, water, lake, ice, mud;

Lightning, rock, sand, nose ornaments of shell, feather apron, football, and gambling bones.

A Miwok infant usually was named by a grandfather or other senior relative, and that name usually referred to one of the totem animals, plants or other objects in his moiety.

With the Miwok, this was not as simple as it sounds. Most names do not mention the totem object directly, but are formed from some verbal or adjectival stem of the totem word. In some cases a name which describes an action or condition might apply to several totem objects, from both the water and land sides. Thus, a boy named ''Slash-claw'' could have been named after a land-side fox or a water-side coyote. The name-giver unquestionably announced the totem reference when he named the baby, and those close to the person thus named knew the name's implication. But a Miwok from another village would not know, in many cases, without an explanation.

To the Miwok, animals were once quasi-humans who occupied the earth before the coming of human beings. It would be an over-simplification to say the Miwok believed man descended from animals. Nor is it correct to suppose that there exists a ''guardian spiritualism'' between a Miwok and the totem animal for which he is named. It would be a mere coincidence, for example, for a man with a coyote-based name to assume, through a series of encounters, dreams or signs, that the coyote was in some way his ''lucky charm'' or even his ''guardian spirit.'' The coyote-named man might just as likely believe he had a special kinship with the bear or eagle or salmon.

The Miwok storyteller, almost invariably a man, was the formal transmitter of the people's culture. The storyteller invariably chose animal characters for his stories in order to save time. Everyone knew the attributes of the animals.

Here is a Miwok story which investigators copied verbatim:

''Two little bears were playing with two little deer. Then, playing that way, the bears said 'You go in!' The little deer went in. 'We'd better say ''maa-maa-maa'' and you let us out' they said. 'All right,' said the bears. Then the bear cubs went in. 'You'd better say ''maa-maa-maa'' ' they said. Then they went in, but they didn't say 'maa'. They died inside there of this smoke.

''When they didn't say 'maa' for a long time (the deer) looked in (and found) both of them had died. Then they took them inside and put them on their bed as if they were asleep. Then their mother smelled their burning hair and came running. She couldn't find her children; she looked everywhere. Then she looked in the bed. When she saw them dead in the bed, she looked for the little deer. She tracked the deer, she tracked them until she found them there in the crack. Then this one, their grandfather, 'Step down, far down,' he said. Then she stepped down a long way, stepping as far as she could reach. When she stepped down to the bottom, he hit her with a hot rock, and killed her. That's all.''

What kind of a person was the Miwok? The tale of the bear and the deer gives no clue, except, perhaps, that you should be prepared to do unto others before they do unto you.

The Miwok was above all peaceable. He rarely hatched plans to harm or rob a neighbor, but he was literally tormented by the belief his neighbor was hatching plans to cause him injury.

Peaceable -- and very suspicious. He did a great deal of muttering. His hatreds smoldered. He only half-concealed his bad will toward those whom he suspected of being his enemies. A favorite daydream was to devise suitable revenge.

He saw no advantage to ending a feud. He rather cherished his hatreds.

Suspicion breeds suspicion and, without a willingness to "bury the hatchet", individual feuds in many cases lasted a lifetime, erupting perhaps only infrequently, but forever smoldering under the surface.

The Miwok had a curious ceremony called the pota which allowed him to take the edge off his hatreds without causing physical damage to the parties involved.

The pota was not for little hates. A murderer of a distant kinsman, the war leader who had said unkind words about one's fighting ability, a shaman thought to have caused an illness through his magic -- these were worthy targets of revenge.

The man giving the pota would invite a great many people to the ceremony -- including the person or persons or their relatives for whom he had a special hate, although not even they knew they were the "guests of honor".

Rude dummies made of tule -- images representing these foes -- were placed in front of the assemblage which then spent the night hurling songs of malevolence and hatred at the effigies.

Later -- a month or a year or several years later -- the pota-giver would make sure his enemy found out that he or his kinsmen had participated in their own reviling.

It would appear that the condition of life -- the compact, relatively static community -- the narrow stage on which the Miwok played out his existence -- formalized even the way he was allowed to hate.

But we must bear in mind that a great many observers reported that, compared to other American natives, the California Indians were a "joyous race". They were considered to be among the "happiest and most gregarious of all American aborigines".

By sifting the various, sometimes contradictory, accounts of the Miwok's personality, our portrait takes on sharpness: The Miwok was contemplative, reserved and very introverted. The innovator had no place in his society. Neither did the egotist, the aggressor, the boaster, the individualist. To be moderate in all things, to act with restraint and dignity -- this was the Miwok ideal.

A prospector wrote in 1850: ''The Indians are really a friendly people unless they are provoked. Unfortunately the Americans frequently treat them unfairly...''

The Sierra foothills are not to be taken for the Garden of Eden. Hunger, wild animals, human predators, the heat of summer, the cold of winter and simply the human condition of those forced to live in too close proximity, were enough to provoke even a race of saints.

The Miwok personality was formed long before the white man appeared. The new invader was merely one more tribulation of nature so far as the Miwok was concerned -- only the white man's tribulation proved nearly fatal.

7

How The Miwok Lived

The Miwok has no migration tales. For all practical purposes he has lived in the foothills and higher reaches of the Sierra Nevada from the beginning of time. He does, however, have an explanation of how some things came to be.

There was a time when the Miwok was without fire. The people were dissatisfied with eating uncooked food and being cold. Then someone discovered people in another locality had fire. The flute-player, mouse, lulled the fire owners to sleep, concealed some coals in his flute and escaped.

Those who sat close to the fire that mouse brought back to the people spoke Miwok. That is, they spoke correctly.

Those who sat far away in the cold could not speak correctly. That is, they spoke the Mono tongue.

There was no Miwok "nation" as such. The village was the main Miwok political unit. There were one hundred and seven known Miwok villages.

The Miwok's relation to the land can be compared to that of a farmer practicing mixed or general agriculture. Each group "farmed" an area of perhaps ten miles long and five miles wide known as a nena -- the Miwok word for "group". The nena usually followed a stream, and it constituted the people's potential for making a living. Some parts of the nena were more productive than others and thus were used more. Harvesting the nena called for a carefully worked out plan, more or less determined by the seasons.

Fishing was good in the rainy winter and spring; hunting prospered in the dry summer and fall. The harvest of acorns -- single most important Miwok commodity -- came in the fall.

Actually, the nena had far deeper significance than group or land. The nena group was a patrilineal (tracing its membership from father to son) joint family. The nena land was the ancestral home in which the lineage supposedly began. Thus the lineage name is always a place name.

The nena had as its head a chief who was, in actual fact, the patriarch of the lineage. Such lineages, in pre-white times, were quasi-political groups, each lineage dwelling at its ancestral home. The men normally brought their wives to their nena; the women of the nena normally married out of the immediate hamlet.

Observers reported in the early part of this century that few Miwoks lived at their nenas -- but every Miwok knew the name of his nena and could pinpoint the ancestral spot from which sprang his patrilineal forebears.

True village life did not come about for the Miwoks until pressure from the white invaders forced nenas to be abandoned, and the refugees gathered with people of many other nenas in the more remote, less disturbed areas.

The Miwok planted no crop except a little tobacco. The only animal he domesticated was the dog. This animal -- the universal protector and hunting companion -- was for the Miwok, in bad times, a hedge against starvation.

Each hamlet, village or main village had a chief who was hereditary and distinctly a civil official. If he commanded in war it was strictly coincidental. The war chief was the village's most distinguished warrior.

If there was no male heir to a chief, the title passed to his female heir. The chieftainess' husband usually was her speaker. The Miwok had head chiefs whose authority was recognized over substantial districts, but each village still had its chief and even sub-chiefs, the latter heading a subsidiary village or acting as speakers and messengers for more important chiefs.

To understand how the village, nena and "nation" functioned one with the other, we must liken the village to a modern city with its own government; the nena to a county containing several "cities"; and the Miwok nation to a politically non-aligned, non-united collection of counties -- the whole held together by the spittle of blood and tradition.

While there was a great deal of dignity attached to the chief's position, his power was limited. Together with the shaman -- if one were available -- the chief found the best sites for gathering acorns. If the trees belonging to another nena were included in the harvest target area, he negotiated the payment for the crop.

The chief made war and peace. That is, he formalized these acts which, in most cases, were brought about by circumstances beyond the control of the participants. War was always waged for revenge, never for plunder.

Revenge for what? For stealing a woman. For killing an intruder. For trespass. For stealing a hanging deer carcass.

The Miwok had no special war instruments. The bow and arrow and spear, weapons for the hunt, were used. In hand-to-hand combat he would pick up a rock and use it as best he could.

War was not waged often or with much enthusiasm. Some authorities

45

say most wars ended with the first casualty. There are reports of skirmishes in which the young boys on both sides were allowed safe passage behind hostile lines to gather spent arrows!

Men captured in warfare were usually killed on the spot. There were no captives except, in some instances, women and children. The Miwok did not know slavery.

Miwok country was traversed by trails -- usually arrow-straight paths regardless of terrain -- not to facilitate the rapid movement of warriors, but to facilitate travel made necessary by the peaceful demands of harvest, hunting and trade.

When trails were hard to follow, the Miwok adopted a quaint custom of hanging a dead skunk adjacent to it to let the nose do what the eye could not.

The Miwok traded with his immediate neighbors. The Northern Miwok supplied the Plains Miwok with finished arrowheads, digger pine nuts, salt and obsidian. In return they received grass seeds and fish from the rich lowlands. The salt mentioned above came from the Washo to the east of the Sierra, and for it the Northern Miwok paid acorns, shell beads, sea shells and baskets.

The Central Miwok traded extensively with the Eastern Mono and the Washo. To these trans-Sierra neighbors he gave shell beads, glass beads, acorns, squaw berries, elderberries, manzanita berries, a fungus used in paint, baskets, sea shells, arrows and soaproot leaves used for brushes. The payment to the Central Miwok included such food delicacies as pine nuts, pandora moth, caterpillars and kutsaui (pupae of the fly), and utilitarian items such as baskets, red paint, white paint, salt, pumice stone, buffalo robes and rabbit-skin blankets.

The Yokuts on the valley floor traded their dogs for Central Miwok blankets and bows and arrows.

The Southern Miwok supplied the Eastern Mono with clam disc beads, and in return received rabbit-skin blankets and basketry materials.

The Miwok dwelling was typically a conical bark house, sometimes with an inner layer of pine needles and an outer layer of earth heaped against the lower reaches. These conical houses were from eight to fifteen feet in diameter, and built without framework or center pole. For a door the Miwok used a smaller slab of bark.

"A man of importance" and his family -- numbering perhaps a dozen people -- might live in a large earth-covered semi-subterranean dwelling. This type of shelter was entered by a ladder through the roof.

In the center of the Miwok house was a fireplace and a small pit, the pit becoming an oven with the addition of hot rocks. The cooking was done both indoors and out, depending on the season, the weather, and what was being prepared.

Miwok slab-bark houses in Yosemite and, at right, an acorn granary.

The people slept on and under mats of skins, usually deerskin, which were laid over the pine-needle carpeted dirt floor.

The chief slept and sat on a bearskin, and he and the well-to-do members of the village might use a willow bed to keep them off the ground.

The rule was one family to a dwelling, although a newlywed and his or her spouse might live in for a time.

The heart of the village was a large semi-subterranean assembly and dance house. This cone-shaped ceremonial structure was built over a large pit, forty or fifty feet in diameter and three or four feet deep. Center poles and beams supported the roof.

The roof was layered in a prescribed manner: the first layer was willow brush laid radially over the horizontal roof timbers. Over this, at right angles, was placed another layer of willow brush. Next came a layer of a thick shrub, followed by a layer of earth, very carefully measured so that it was always four to five inches thick.

In the ceremonial house was a drum -- another of those devices by which white men rank the cultures of the world's native populations. The drum

47

Stereoptican photo of a cluster of Miwok houses on the Fremont Rancho near Mariposa.

was large -- a five- or ten-foot section of hollowed log -- placed over a three-foot-deep pit resonance chamber. Both ends of the log were left open. It was played with the foot, the drummer standing and stamping and steadying himself by holding on to a nearby pole.

The Miwok sweat house, also a conical earth-covered structure built over a shallow pit, was much smaller than the assembly house. Ten men in a half-erect position could fit into the larger sweat houses.

Each man brought his own pile of wood to burn on the fire to induce the heat necessary for sweating. The size of the wood pile determined the man's strength -- the more wood, the hotter the fire; the hotter the fire, the stronger the man. Or at least that was how the Miwok figured it.

The idea was to sweat for an hour or so -- starting before sunrise -- and then jump into a nearby creek or river; return to the sweat house for another session of heat -- then back into the water.

Sweating purified the man -- especially the hunter about to chase deer -- and very especially the deer hunter who was up against a run of bad luck.

With the Miwok, sweating was not merely superstition having to do with purifying the body. Bad luck in deer hunting usually was a matter of the hunter's legs giving out. Sweating took out the kinks.

While the main association of the sweat house was with preparation for deer hunting, it was also used by men suffering from rheumatism or by men about to dance in a ceremony.

In the summer an assembly house made of brush would be built for ceremonials, especially a mourning anniversary. This house was circular

Three Miwok roundhouses and an outbuilding, in the rancheria on the ridge north of Murphys. Fire leveled these structures in 1922.

and roofed with brush and pine needles. It too was much smaller than the semi-subterranean assembly house.

The Miwok also built sun shelters and grinding booths, the latter simple bark-and-brush affairs over a bedrock mortar or imbedded portable mortar.

The Miwok stored acorns in carefully constructed granaries shaped like inverted cones, some 12 feet high and rather resembling huge bird nests. These were made of poles, twigs and brush, lined with weeds and grass and so tightly constructed that they sometimes were used to store grass seed. The whole was covered so as to make the storehouse water-tight through the winter.

Another view of the roundhouses near Murphys. Photo was taken in October, 1906.

Each family had at least one granary. The important men in the village--those who would be called upon to sponsor feasts -- had several. The granaries were sometimes miles from the place where their owners lived.

The Miwok had few material possessions. What we do know about his tools and ornaments comes from S. A. Barrett and E. W. Gifford's *Miwok Material Culture,* published in 1933. Dr. Barrett was director of the Milwaukee Public Museum and did field work among the Pomo and Miwok while a resident of the state and later as a student of Kroeber's at the University of California. Gifford taught at U.C. and did considerable field work with the California Indians. Both are deceased. Even observations made just prior to 1933 came too late for us to know the complete Miwok story. In many cases, the observers had to rely on old men or hearsay for information on certain subjects.

The Miwok made no portable mortars, according to Barrett and Gifford, and those they used were found by them -- made for The People, they believed, by Coyote, a supernatural being. From the evidence at hand -- considerable local collections of metates in all stages of development, from just-started depressions to deep-holed affairs -- there is reason to question the early observers on this particular point. Indeed, Sierra Nevada old-timers tell of an abundance of portable mortars -- so many, in fact, that they were used as underground footings or sockets for fence gates.

One cannot argue, however, with the Barrett-Gifford observation that it was more sociable to pulverize food in a bedrock mortar near a stream. Any appropriately-shaped stone served as a pestle.

The Miwok used acorn crackers -- merely small roundish stones that fitted nicely in the hands and did the job for which they were intended.

Oaken bowls and pottery vessels were made by the Western Mono, and a few found their way into Miwok territory. The Miwok did make some clay figures of animals, but this does not qualify as pottery.

The Miwok quarried steatite (soapstone), which was used for cooking stones. The hot stones were placed directly into the baskets of uncooked food. Steatite sometimes was found in the shape of a bowl, and the Miwok used these directly over an open fire.

The Miwok made abundant use of chipped stone, especially obsidian, flint and jasper which flake into sharp points. These the Miwok used for knives, arrow points and spear points.

Two types of arrow straighteners were employed. A perforated straightener, made of manzanita, stone or maple, had a hole through which a heated arrow was inserted and straightened. A grooved steatite stone also was used in this work.

The awl used in coiling baskets was made of deer bone. Whistles used in ceremonials were made of jackrabbit and grouse limb bones. Antler points

Soaproot brushes used as meal and hair brushes. Top center one is ready for pitch and handle. Two lower corner ones are very old and used.

were used to flake arrow points and other obsidian objects, and to extract acorns stored by woodpeckers.

From the soaproot the Miwok made an all-purpose brush for the hair and to scrub cooking baskets.

When a Miwok went to war, he kicked off his moccasins, slipped on a fur forehead band on a special cap of grass, and took up his bow and arrow and spear.

The bow usually was made of spruce or incense cedar, or, in the lower elevations, from ash trees. The Miwok backed their bows with deer sinew.

Bow-making was a specialized trade, and the bow-maker was also the arrow-maker. The Miwok used two kinds of arrows. One, a simple shaft, was for small game. The second, for war and big game, had a foreshaft with arrowpoint, attached to the main shaft by an adhesive which would melt from the heat of the animal or man that had been shot. Thus the arrow would remain in the body of the victim even if the arrow shaft was pulled out or broken off.

The arrow base was painted red and fitted with feathers, usually of the Western red-tail hawk.

The Miwok had two kinds of quivers. One of buckskin remained in the

Obsidian and flint arrowpoints and blades.

From top to bottom: Sinew-backed bow, Calaveras County. Arrow with obsidian point. Two arrows. Digging stick for roots and bulbs, probably the Miwoks' most valuable tool.

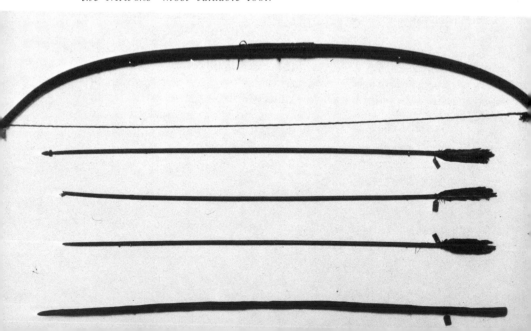

home. The carrying quiver was made from the skin of a black fox, otter or dog.

Stephen Powers reported in 1877 that Miwok of both sexes and all ages went absolutely naked. This observation probably was made during a heat wave. In point of fact the Miwok, after about ten years of age, did wear clothing.

The man wore a buckskin breech clout that passed between the legs and hung from a buckskin girdle. The appearance was of a short apron, front and back.

Like women in all places and at all times, there was some variation, at least between localities, in women's wear.

The Northern Miwok women wore a sarong-like buckskin wrapping about the loins reaching to mid-way between ankle and knee. These garments were fringed.

The Central Miwok women copied this dress, adding a buckskin band across each shoulder. They also wore a second outfit -- a two-piece dress. The back apron was put on first, with the front apron overlapping it.

In warmer weather, the Central Miwok women wore a buckskin clout, similar to that worn by men, over which they donned a waist-to-knee grass skirt.

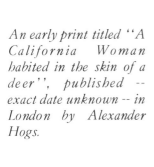

An early print titled "A California Woman habited in the skin of a deer", published -- exact date unknown -- in London by Alexander Hogs.

In cold weather, the people wore fur blankets usually made from woven rabbit fur, and also from mountain lion, deer, bear, coyote or other animals. Buffalo skin blankets came by trade from east of the Sierra. The rarest Miwok blanket was made from duck or goose feathers.

The surest sign of Miwok wealth was a belt made from the scalps of California woodpeckers sewn on a buckskin strip and fringed with olive shell disks.

Moccasin-making was man's work. Deerskin footwear was used only in cold weather or for rough-country travel.

The Miwok commonly wore flowers in his hair -- especially showy flowers. The hair was worn long and only cut and hidden, buried or burned with the corpse of a near relative, as a sign of mourning. It was considered dangerous to have one's hair fall into the hands of a shaman who harbored evil intent. The shaman could concoct an illness over the hair.

String of olivella shells.
Calaveras County.

Miwok men and women practiced tattooing. The usual decoration extended from the lower lip to the navel.

The Miwok rarely painted his body except for ceremonials. Three colors were used: black (charcoal), white (chalk), and red (mineral pigment).

All Miwok children had their ears and nasal septum pierced, and the openings made progressively larger with grass stems.

Both men and women wore earrings and earplugs. Women favored earrings and men earplugs -- but both sexes wore ornamentation only on ceremonial occasions, unless the person was wealthy or important or both. Then the ornaments were worn at all times.

The Miwok's idea of a well-shaped head was one that was flat in the back, brought about by a proper upbringing on a hard cradle; and a short and flat forehead, which the mother molded by pressing and rubbing the infant's head from center to sides. In addition, the nose was flattened by pressing, and the eyebrows rubbed apart.

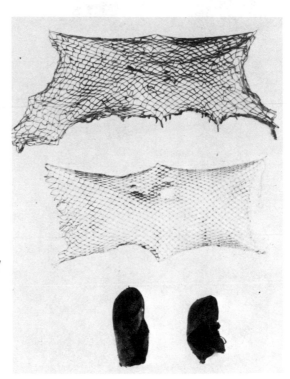

A pair of sandals and headnets.

The California Indian did win the world's acclaim for his basketry. While the Miwok's work is coarser than that of neighboring tribes, it was nonetheless outstanding. The Miwok basket was a plain affair, rarely decorated.

The Miwok raised their infants in cradle boards, and here we have a marked difference in style among the dialect groupings. The Northern Miwok cradle was made of two hooked oaken sticks bound across with slats. The Southern Miwok used a woven cradle made of willow warp.

Milkweed fiber string was the material used for making fish nets as well as a netting bag for carrying bulbs and corms. For cordage the Miwok used a withe of grapevine or a grass stem. String was made from various bast fibers, most notably milkweeed.

The Miwok boat, used in lagoons and on the rivers, was a tule balsa --

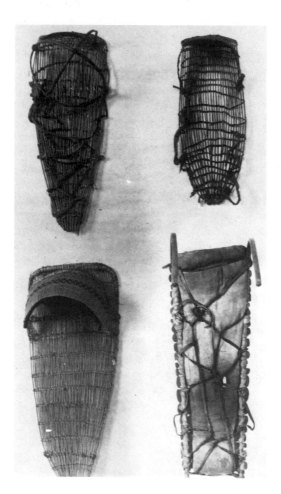

Miwok cradles from Calaveras and Mariposa counties, showing wide variety of design. Photographed in April, 1909.

While the Miwok were not famous for their baskets, their weaving was adequate, as this example shows. Photo taken in 1906.

about twenty cylindrical bundles of tule about fifteen feet in length and four feet wide. Willow ribs were used for rigidity, and paddles for propulsion.

The Miwok used beads and shells in necklaces, belts, bandoliers and shell ropes. They made few of these articles, mostly obtaining them in trade. Dances and ceremonies -- or in death when ornamentation was placed on the corpse -- were the times for bead wearing. In the mid-1960's graveyards in the Jamestown area in Central Miwok country were desecrated, for a time flooding local antique and second-hand stores with heavy yields of beads. The Tuolumne County Sheriff put an end to this traffic.

The Costanoans of Monterey Bay allowed Miwok passage for the purpose of gathering abalone pectorals and olive shells, but olive shell disk beads usually came into Miwok hands by way of people from the south. By baking the shells the Miwok obtained the color he wanted: white. The natural lustrous grays and browns had no appeal to the mountain Indians. Clam shell beads filtered into Miwok country from the northwest.

The Miwok did not count his shell bead money -- he measured it. A lua of shell bead money was a string reaching from the nipple to the end of the outstretched arm on the opposite side of the body. An ana was the distance between the outstretched arms. The yana was the length of a man. This latter measurement also was used in determining the diameter of a circular ceremonial house, always given in so many yanas.

Currency included shell beads, baskets, acorns and flicker feather headbands.

57

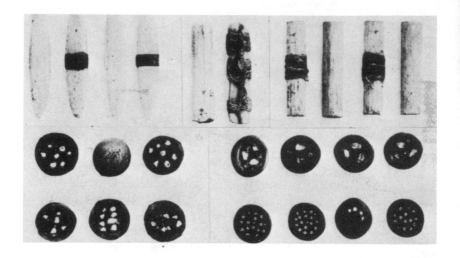

Gambling bones and dice which were very popular with the Miwoks. The latter are actually Yokuts dice but are very similar to those used by Miwoks.

"An Indian is ten days in making a bow, and it is valued at $3, $4 and $5, according to the workmanship, an arrow at 12½ cents," wrote Powers. "Three kinds of money were employed in this traffic. White shell-buttons, pierced in the center and strung together, rate at $5 a yard (this money was less valuable among the Nishinam, probably because these lived nearer the source of supply); 'periwinkles' at $1 a yard; fancy marine shells at various prices, from $3 to $10 or $15 a yard, according to their beauty."

The Miwok dog is described by Barrett and Gifford as being brindled, medium-sized, prick-eared, short-haired, curled tailed, and muzzled like a coyote. Dogs were rare and valuable in Miwok country. The rarity is due to two factors: The food to feed dogs was scarce; the dog itself was occasionally food to the Miwok.

It was not all work and no play for the Miwok adult. Indeed, the Miwok's love for gaming put him in low esteem with many church-bent observers. If the California Indian was nothing else, he was a gambler.

The Indian's guessing games and dice games were rarely no-stake affairs. The contestants agreed on the amount of the bet and the means of determining a winner, and off they went -- sometimes for days! It is interesting to note how the Indian tallied his score. Because the contests were for a pre-determined wager -- not for continuing antes and individual hand bets -- the game would start with ten or twelve or whatever number of markers (usually sticks or pebbles) the contestants agreed on. These were placed in the "pot" controlled by a third party who was forbidden to make any sidebets on the action. As one or another contestant won a hand, the pot guardian gave the winner a tally until all were gone. Then the play continued with loser passing a tally directly to the winner until one or the other had them all. When this happened, the game was over, and the original bet was paid off, with the pot guardian receiving a small percentage for his efforts.

The men played "hand game" or "grass game" which required two pairs of four-inch-long bones, one of each pair notched and wrapped about its middle with a sinew string, the other pair unmarked. The game was played with two men on a side, each placing a bone, concealed in bunches of grass or pine needles, in his closed hand. The players with the bones would rotate their hands in front of their chests, all the while singing their gambling songs -- a bit of psychological warfare whose intent it was to confuse the opponents.

Finally, the guesses would be made -- this hand had the wrapped -- or unwrapped -- bone. If neither guess was correct, the bone holders would get two markers and another turn. If both guesses were right, the guessers would get two markers and the next chance to hide the bones. If only one guess was right, the guessers received one counter -- but the bone-holder incorrectly guessed had another turn.

The women's guessing game was practically the same, the chief difference being in the ritual of displaying the closed hand. The women folded their arms so that their hands were hidden in their armpits.

The stick game was strictly for males in which one man would hold forty-four small sticks in his left hand and then, without warning, grab hold of a number of them in his right, which then quickly went behind his back. The opponent would guess one, two, three or four. The sticks were counted in fours, and if the remainder was the number guessed, the guesser received the sticks. If it was either of the other three numbers, the guesser lost his original bet, which undoubtedly was given to him at four-to-one odds.

The women were the dice throwers among the Miwok. The die was half an acorn meat, or half cylinders of wood. Four, six or eight dice were shaken by hand and tossed onto a flat surface. There were only two ways to score in this game: if all the dice ended up all flat or all round side up the thrower received two points; if an equal number of flat and rounded sides were up, one point.

It would appear that the Miwok games were strictly games of blind chance. Who, for instance, can guess if the hand holds a notched or an unnotched bone if the distribution is made out of sight under a buckskin, as was the case in the women's games?

And yet, the Miwok had very good gamblers, good gamblers, fair gamblers, and poor gamblers. The very good gamblers were masters of psychology. They knew their opponents. They knew a man's mental patterns -- if he holds the notched bone in his right hand three times in a row, he will not chance a fourth straight time. And they knew how to read body movements and habits. And what modern-day dice thrower has not tried to make today's perfectly tooled cubes "behave" in certain favorable ways? A downright impossibility, and yet they persist in trying. The Miwok's dice were simpler. Instead of six surfaces, they had but two. Perhaps spending the leisure time of one's lifetime casting dice of this type could lead to techniques that separated the women from the girls.

When we understand the spirit of the guessing game and other gambling games, we begin to understand the spirit of the Miwok.

A gesture begun in one way can be finished in another, if in the split-second of executing the gesture one recognizes on the face of his opponent a trace of satisfaction over the impending false guess.

"These attempts to provoke betrayal imply instantaneous shiftings of features and fingers and lightninglike decisions and reactions," wrote Anthropologist Kroeber.

From this evidence, he continued, "it is impossible to have seen a Californian Indian warmed to his work in this game when played for stakes -- provided its aim and method are understood -- and any longer justly to designate him mentally sluggish and emotionally apathetic, as is the wont."

The game does not depend on sticks and luck, "but the tensest of wills, the keenest perceptions, and the supplest of muscular responses are matched; and only rarely are the faculties of a Caucasian left sufficiently undulled in adult age to compete other than disastrously against the Indian practiced in his specialty.

"Seen in this light, the contortions, gesticulations, noises, and excitement of the native are not the mere uncontrolledness of an overgrown child, but the outward reflexes of a powerfully surcharged intensity, and devices that at once stimulate the contestant's energy still further and aid him in dazzling and confusing his opponent. There is possibly no game in the world that, played sitting, has, with equal intrinsic simplicity, such competitive capacities."

The chief work of children is play, and the Miwok child was no exception. He had toys -- tops, buzzers, musical strings -- made of acorns. And like the grownups, the youngsters played a guessing game -- and they also made wagers. They used a single piece of charcoal, and the other side's chore was to guess which hand was "it".

The more active games included the universal favorite, hide-and-go-seek, except instead of one seeker and many hiders, the Miwok employed

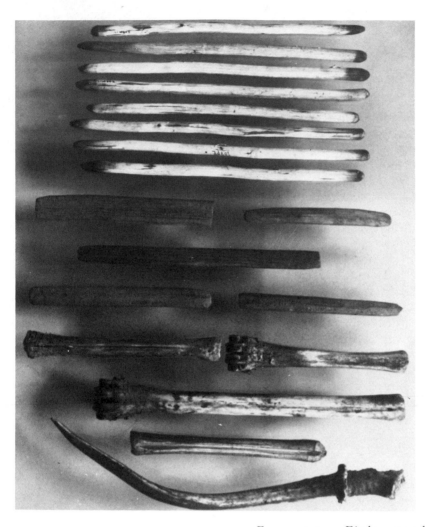

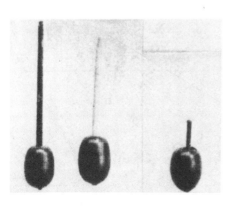

From top: Eight wooden counters used with bones in plate game. Five mesh sticks for net-making. Four leg bones of deer, partly worked and polished, to be used in making gambling bones. A deer antler implement used to extract acorns from the bark of trees, where they had been placed by woodpeckers.

Acorn tops which were popular toys of the Miwok children.

61

many seekers and only one hider. When the search failed, the hider called out and the last searcher to return to home base was "it" -- that is, he became the hider. If the hider was found, he had to hide again. With such an arrangement -- always bearing in mind the Miwok's tight communal life -- what implications can modern psychologists draw from this game? The white child's "reward" is to become one of the hiders. No one relishes the role of being a lonely, solitary seeker of a bevy of hiding peers who have every advantage except proximity to the base but who need not make their move toward the base and its immunity until the seeker commits himself. The Miwok places the security of numbers with the seekers -- the hunters. The hider is isolated.

Ululu was a game children played by forming a long line and "following the leader" until one of the children sang out. The children then would turn in his direction, until someone else sang out, and the participants turned toward him. The object was to be facing the last person to sing out, that is, facing in the "right" direction.

Miwok children played tag games, including "last tag". This game was usually the finale to a busy day of play as the youngsters were heading to their respective homes. A child who was "last tagged" was not supposed to look upon the tagger. His job was to tag someone else and thus gain temporary immunity.

Miwok adults played field games, and competed in archery and spear-throwing contests.

Southern Miwok men played shinney with wooden sticks and an oak ball about the size of a billiard ball. The area of play was about the size and shape of a modern football field. The object of the game was to hit the ball through the goal. From two to a dozen or more men participated.

Women's shinney was similar to the men's game, except the stick was pointed rather than curved or clubbed on the end; and instead of a ball, a two-foot diameter rope ring was used.

Field for women's basketball game.

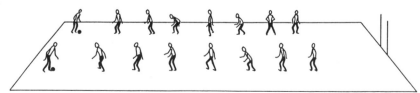

Field for men's football game.

Rackets and leather and wooden balls used by Miwoks in their games.

Women and girls also played basketball -- that is, they used a very small buckskin ball which they moved in handled baskets resembling seed beaters. The ball could not be touched by hand -- it had to be carried in the baskets or thrown forward from a basket -- toward the goal. The field was about two hundred yards long. A player running with the ball in her basket could be tackled by the opponents.

The women also competed in sakumship in which two players, standing fifty feet apart, played "catch" with a four-inch buckskin ball thrown with a casting basket and caught with a catching basket. Hands could not touch the ball. Score was kept of the number of misses or bad throws.

Men or boys played "football" on a field about fifty yards long, with a single goal post at one end only. Each of the two sides, sometimes numbering as many as twenty-five participants, took their positions in two parallel lines stretching from the kickoff line to the goal post. When the signal was given, each side kicked its eight-inch buckskin ball down its line, from one kicker to the next, toward the goal. Only feet could be used to move the ball, and the first side to kick its ball through the goal was winner.

Many other games were played, including one in which darts were tossed through moving hoops.

In nearly all the games heavy wagering took place, both by the participants and the spectators. There were no umpires or referees as such. The Miwok audience ruled on close decisions.

In some of the contests there seems not to have been special groupings for teams along moiety lines. The women's shinney game, for instance, tended to match women from one village against those of another. In basketball, on the other hand, the usual grouping was water people against land people.

A few Miwok gaming artifacts can be seen in museums, along with some very humble work tools, articles of clothing and ceremonial paraphernalia.

However, the one tool that separated the Miwok and his fellow California Indians from all other aborigines on earth, save perhaps those in Australia and New Guinea, the tool that was to the stone age what the computer is to the space age, was the digging stick that gave the California Indian his name: "Digger". It was three to four feet long and usually shaped from mountain mahogany or buck brush. The point was hardened by fire. The idea was to hold the stick with both hands and jab it into the ground to dig a bulb out of the hard, red mountain ground.

Barrett and Gifford concede that the digging stick was "more effective than a steel spade, for only the minimum quantity of earth was moved."

The museums have a few digging sticks. They are the true cross of the California Indian -- the stake upon which their reputation as humans was impaled.

8

Food Is Life

"I know. You want to know about the time when we were little children.

"Of my father I know nothing . But my mother I remember would spread out acorns to dry in the sun, and later she would pound them, after winnowing them she would grind them fine with a pestle. The acorn mush they would eat with mushrooms, eat it soft from the hand. With yellow mushrooms and with ground-squirrel meat they would eat the acorn bread. Gray squirrel they would eat, quail they would eat, rats and wood rats, all the people would eat. My father would shoot ground squirrels and eat them himself. They would take yellowjackets' nests, and they would eat them with acorn bread.

"My grandmother would pound acorns, and my grandfather would fish for salmon. The people ate deer meat then. And they ate a mush made of all kinds of seeds. They would grind the seeds, and then mash them in a deep mortar; then they would roll it in a ball and cook it. They would cook cabbage, too, and then leach it in water..."

Ever member of the community worked hard. A subsistence existence is a hard existence, but hard is not necessarily bad. Life revolved around that which sustained and nurtured life: food. And the surfeit or lack of food was determined by the seasons, and by the rhythm of the universe.

The time of greatest hunger was when the indoor work of winter was completed, the food stores were gone or nearly gone, and there was no hint of spring. What good then was an occasional ground squirrel or a mushroom when a man had hunger enough to eat a deer?

This was the time -- the deepest and darkest moment before the dawn -- when the very old and the very young suffered most. They were the most vulnerable to the ravages of diminished nourishment. The futile and empty sounds of mourning and suffering were companions to the deep silence of winter.

But, as always, there came a day when the sun was capable of warming the body and the rain did not sting with cold. And suddenly, miraculously, the red clay mud earth was a green carpet of clover and the streams were alive with fish.

Spring was the time of feasting -- of eating as much as one wanted in the knowledge that the curve was ever upward: even better days lay ahead. The village was rediscovered as a beautiful, green, warm place. Other villages were visited. Ceremonies and dances, lasting for days, brought the people together. And, with good venison and tender bulbs in plentiful supply, there were the makings of feasts to be enjoyed by family and intimate friends.

The intense heat of summer slowed the mid-day pace. Life moved out of doors -- under the shade of thatched shelter. The work of gathering food -- in summer seeds were harvested -- and of hunting, took place in the early morning or long twilight hours. This was the time for short migrations into the higher country where hunting was better and the air cooler.

The Miwok and his California neighbors were the most omnivorous aborigines in North America. While the acorn was his staple, it did not have the same exclusive position in his life-sustaining scheme of things that, for instance, corn, salmon, buffalo, reindeer or seal had in other areas.

"Where the acorn abounded," wrote Kroeber (*Handbook of Indians of California*), "the practices both of collecting and of treating it led directly to the utilization also of other sources of nourishment. The farmer may and does hunt, or fish, or gather wild growths; but these activities, being of a different order, are a distraction from his regular pursuits, and an adjustment is necessary."

The Miwok, not being a farmer, gathered and hunted as a regular pursuit, and in a sense he gathered everything and hunted everything that was edible. If, for instance, the day's goal was to fish for trout, but the fishing party came across fresh deer tracks, the goal was quickly changed. The securing of plant food is essentially the same as securing grasshoppers or maggots or caterpillars. A digging stick thrust into the ground in the hopes of unearthing a bulb could just as likely unearth an edible worm.

"The food sources of California were bountiful in their variety rather than in their overwhelming abundance," wrote Kroeber. "If one supply failed, there were a hundred others to fall back upon."

Not so where aborigines depended on a single staple: "If a drouth withered the corn shoots, if the buffalo unaccountably shifted, or the salmon failed to run, the very existence of peoples in other regions was shaken to its foundations. But the manifold distribution of available foods in California and the working out of corresponding means of reclaiming them prevented a failure of the acorn crop from producing similar effects. It might produce short rations and racking hunger, but scarcely starvation."

At no time of year did the Miwok eat meals at regular times, except the sunrise breakfast. The Miwok had several eating and cooking habits which

This Miwok woman, named Ta-Bu-Ce, holds a basket of acorn meal. The photo was taken a half-century ago in Yosemite.

produced mixed reactions in white observers. The Indian ate when he was hungry, and the first thing he did when he had guests was to feed them, no matter what time of day or night the visitors arrived. Fingers -- and very rarely a river mussel shell -- were used as eating utensils.

The Miwok cooked food in several ways: by boiling in a steatite vessel over an open flame; by boiling in a basket by introducing hot stones; by baking or steaming in an earth oven; by parching with hot coals; and by broiling or roasting over coals and hot ashes.

The dried meat baskets were nearly filled when the first nip of autumn tempered the hot summer days and nights. Now the people harvested plums and cherries and anticipated the dropping of the acorn, their chief food source.

The coming of the cool weather signaled the time for coming together. The people created acorn harvest encampments which were relaxed, friendly, neighborly and gossipy -- in contrast to the spring clover harvest, which had an edge of frenetic excitement brought about by the release from winter. Autumn was the time for friends beyond the family circle. It was during the autumn that one became acquainted with people from other villages, and even with foreigners on trade and hunting expeditions.

Theodora Kroeber, describing the Yana, a foothill people to the north of the Miwok, wrote: "What the men and women and children learned

Acorn caches at Railroad Flat, Calaveras County.

Acorn cache near an Indian Village in Yosemite Valley.

68

and experienced during the days of the big encampments would be the raw material for conversation, speculation, and philosophizing after everyone was home again, and the days drew in: the odd names by which people and tools were called; a different way of shooting a bow; a song of another people.''

The harvest encampment and autumn, too, ended with the first cold rain of winter. Now came the days of cold -- the time for work within the house, for there was time now to repair bows and arrows and make baskets, mats, cordage, nets, beads, knives, points, paddles, and brushes. It was the time of the storyteller, who carried the Miwok culture forward into the new generations.

Winter was a good time, too -- if it did not last beyond the time the food baskets were empty and the dry firewood too great a distance from the home fire. The new clover slept under the ground, but it did not sleep forever. Its awakening brought the Miwok year to full circle.

The Miwok ate almost everything edible in the vegetable world. The same applies to the animal world, with the exception of the turkey vulture and, among the Central Miwok, the bear, whose foot ''looks too human.''

Black oak acorns, *Godetia viminea* seeds, venison and the flesh of the California gray squirrel were at the top of the Miwok epicurean list.

After acorns and seeds (the latter sometimes considered delicacies), the vegetable food preference in descending order was mushrooms, corms, bulbs and, lastly, manzanita berries. The buckeye fruit was strictly starvation rations.

The Miwok ate coyote, dog, skunk, mountain lion, wildcat, snakes, frogs and lizards. There was some variation from village to village as to who ate what, but in general the more exotic foods (especially snakes, frogs and lizards) were favored by the elderly.

The eating of insects was a Miwok food habit which white observers were very much prone to comment upon. Grasshoppers were driven into pits by large groups of people -- sometimes several villages participating in one drive. The grasshoppers were either cooked in an earth oven or parched in an openwork basket. Cocoons, probably of the Army Worm, were steamed in the earth oven, or boiled, or sun-dried and saved for winter. Chrysalids of the Pandora Moth were parched. A green worm was squeezed out and steamed. Yellowjacket larvae also were eaten.

The Miwok made meal from seeds, eaten either dry, as cakes, or cooked into a mush. These seeds came from grasses, small plants and shrubs, and were gathered by means of a conical burden basket and a handled seed beater. Seed, according to Barrett and Gifford, was regarded as particullarly fine fare. ''Visitors were given it to eat along with their acorn mush, which was regarded as insipid without such accompaniment.''

Seed beater, at right, and openwork baskets.

Barrett and Gifford list seventeen identified species of nut- and seed-bearing plants (other than acorn and buckeye) which provided food for the Miwok:

Oats *(Avena barbata)* -- were pounded lightly in a mortar merely to loosen the husks, not to pulverize the seeds. Then followed winnowing. After that the seeds were parched with coals in a basket. The seeds were next pulverized in a mortar, and finally stone-boiled in a basket, making a soup or mush.

Balsam Root *(Balsamorrhiza sagittata)* -- seeds were cracked with mortar and pestle, winnowed and eaten.

Dense-Flowered Evening Primrose *(Boisduvalia densiflora)* -- seeds were gathered with a seed-beater and burden basket, parched, pulverized, and eaten dry. Those stored were unparched.

Upright Evening Primrose *(Boisduvalia stricta)* -- seeds were gathered in the fall, parched and pulverized, and the meal eaten dry.

"Ripgut" Grass *(Bromus rigidus)* -- seeds were pulverized and eaten as pinole (dried, ground or sweetened corn or wheat).

Red Maids *(Calandrinia caulescens)* -- the prized seed from this small plant was very rich and oily; it was eaten pulverized. In late May the entire plant was pulled up and spread out to dry. The seeds, separated from the plants, were gathered and placed in a tightly coiled flat-bottomed basket and winnowed. The seeds were prepared by parching in a basket plate and then pulverized. The oily meal was pressed into balls and cakes for eating.

Painted Cup *(Castilleia)* -- seeds were gathered in June, then dried and stored for winter. They were parched, pounded and eaten dry.

Fitch's Spikeweed *(Centromedia fitchii)* -- seeds were eaten as mush.

Clarkia *(Clarkia elegans)* -- seeds were dried, and then parched and pulverized in a mortar. The meal was eaten with acorn mush.

Hazel *(Corylus rostrata)* -- nuts were used to a limited extent as food.

Summer's Darling *(Godetia amoena)* -- as with Red Maids, the whole plant was pulled up and dried to remove the seeds, which were parched, pulverized and eaten dry.

Farewell to Spring *(Godetia biloba)* -- tops of the plants were harvested in June, dried on granite outcrops, and the seeds removed by treading and beating with sticks. After winnowing, the seeds were stored in baskets. They were parched and pulverized before eating.

Farewell to Spring *(Godetia viminea)* -- the entire plants were pulled up, bound in sheaves, placed in water for two hours, and laid on a granite outcrop to dry. The seeds were released by beating the pods with sticks. After winnowing and storage, the seeds were pulverized, but eaten dry and uncooked.

Gum-Weed *(Madia dissitiflora)* -- seeds were harvested in August, winnowed and stored. To prepare this valued food, the seeds were parched with coals in a parching basket, rewinnowed, and then pulverized in a mortar, creating an oily meal.

Tarweed *(Madia elegans)* -- seeds were gathered in midsummer, winnowed, pulverized in a bedrock mortar. The meal was eaten dry.

Chile Tarweed *(Madia sativa)* -- seeds eaten directly as food.

Buena Mujer *(Mentzelia)* -- seeds pulverized and eaten as pinole.

Skunkweed *(Navarretia)* -- seeds gathered in August, sun-dried and stored, then parched and pulverized and eaten dry.

Valley Tassels *(Orthocarpus attenuatus)* -- seeds gathered with seed-beater and burden basket, dried, parched, pulverized and eaten dry.

California Buttercup *(Ranunculus californicus)* -- seeds gathered in June, winnowed, dried, stored, and then parched and pulverized in a bedrock mortar.

Of course there were many more seed plants utilized, but the Miwok informants and the white man scientists could not match the one's descriptions with the other's Latin names.

The Miwok ate a wide variety of roots, corms, tubers and bulbs which are commonly referred to as ''Indian potatoes.'' Gathered by means of the digging stick, this food was baked or steamed in the earth oven, roasted in ashes, or stone-boiled in baskets. After baking, some ''Indian potatoes'' were stored for winter use. These were placed in baskets in the home.

A dozen kinds of ''potatoes'' were identified by Barrett and Gifford:

Ookow *(Brodiaea pulchella)* -- steamed in the earth oven.

Harvest Brodiaea *(Brodiaea coronaria)* -- dug about the first of May, the exact time determined by the chief. Both men and women went on a four-day excursion and picnic to gather up these bulbs, which were transported to the cooking place, where they were prepared in earth ovens on the fourth day.

White Brodiaea *(Brodiaea hyacinthina)* -- bulbs were dug from a depth of several inches and steamed in the earth oven.

Golden Brodiaea *(Brodiaea ixioides)* -- bulbs were eaten.

"Nigger-Toe" *(Brodiaea)* -- cooked and eaten.

Grass Nuts *(Brodiaea)* -- eaten.

White Mariposa Lily *(Calochortus venustus)* -- bulbs were dug when buds appeared on the plant in April, roasted for about twenty minutes in the ashes of a fire that had died down. When extracted they were soft, like boiled potatoes.

Squaw-Root *(Carum gairdneri)* -- boiled and eaten like a potato.

Anise *(Carum kelloggii)* -- eaten.

Soaproot *(Chlorogalum pomeridianum)* -- root was wilted and rubbed to remove the dried outer leaf parts, and then baked in the earth oven. Bulbs were dried without baking for winter use. The Soaproot was a valuable plant to the Miwok. It was used not only for food but as fish poison, detergent, glue and for brushes.

Eulophus *(Eulophus bolanderi)* -- cooked by stone-boiling, peeled and eaten. This plant served as a substitute for acorn when that commodity was much reduced or depleted, as was likely to occur in summer before the acorn harvest began. When so used, the Eulophus was washed, sun-dried, and pounded in a bedrock mortar.

St. John's Wort *(Hypericum formosum)* -- eaten fresh from the ground, or dried, ground into flour, and used like acorn meal.

Corn Lily *(Veratrum californicum)* -- roasted in hot ashes, peeled, and eaten. It was not stored.

Mushrooms were shredded and dried, and then boiled and eaten with salt, or cooked in soups.

Elizabeth Benton Fremont, Col. John C. Fremont's daughter, provides us with a bit of humorous insight into the mushroom vis-a-vis the Miwok.

The year was 1858. The place: the Fremonts' 43,000-acre Mariposa Ranch.

"One day the squaws were returning from the fields," wrote Miss Fremont, "when my mother noticed that their baskets were filled with a mixture of mushrooms and toadstools. By means of a sign language and a few Mexican words, mother explained to the women that the toadstools would kill them, and in order to illustrate this to them, she put some of the toadstools in a sauce pan, cooked them and dropped in a piece of silver, to show them how the poisonous mass blackened the bright silver. The squaws watched the process with much interest, and then the spokeswoman of the party replied:

" 'Kill white woman; not kill Indian,' and taking a liberal portion of the toadstools, smiled and said: 'Come tomorrow.'

"The woman did come 'tomorrow,' the toadstools apparently having not the slightest effect upon her."

On the Mariposa, Miss Fremont added, the friendliest relations always existed between the Indians and the Fremonts -- "my father permitting no one to disturb them in their ranches or at their springs."

The Indian women made seats for themselves near the Fremont Ranch kitchen, and gathered there at noontime.

"Their favorite lunch," wrote Miss Fremont, "consisted of a sandwich made of bread, suet and turnip peelings, and we always made it a point to have a supply of these dainties ready for them."

The buckeye nut was extremely difficult to process into food because of the great amount of leaching necessary to remove the tannin. The nuts were gathered and stored and only used if the acorn crop failed.

The Miwok ate pine nuts, and especially valued the nuts of the digger pine and sugar pine. The Indians made great use of these and other conifers. Needles were used for thatch, bedding and floor covering; bark for house covering; and twigs and rootlets for sewing material for coiled baskets.

Barrett and Gifford identified two dozen plants the Miwok ate as greens, although they used still another dozen plants whose exact identity is lost.

The following greens were eaten either raw, after stone-boiling in a basket, or after steaming in the earth oven. The usual practice was to eat greens as an accompaniment to acorn soup.

Here is Barrett and Gifford's list of identifiable Miwok greens and notes of interest:

Columbine *(Aquilegia truncata)* -- boiled; early spring.

Milkweed *(Asclepias mexicana)* -- boiled. Sometimes added to manzanita cider to thicken it.

White Goosefoot *(Chenopodium album)* -- boiled. Sometimes dried and stored for later use.

Western Larkspur *(Delphinium hesperium)* -- leaves and flowers boiled.

Larkspur *(Delphinium)* -- boiled in March when young.

Horseweed *(Erigeron canadensis)* -- leaves and tender tops pounded in the bedrock mortar. Eaten pulverized, but uncooked. Flavor like onions.

Tibinagua *(Eriogonum nudum)* -- eaten raw. Sour flavor.

Alum Root *(Heuchera micrantha)* -- leaves first to be eaten in spring. Boiled or steamed. After steaming a certain quantity might be dried and stored.

Wild Pea *(Lathyrus vestitus)* -- eaten as greens; seeds eaten raw.

Rose Lupine *(Lupinus densiflorus)* -- early in spring its leaves and flowers are stripped from the stalk and then steamed in the earth oven. This plant was regarded as common daily food.

Broad-Leaved Lupine *(Lupinus latifolius)* -- leaves and flowers steamed in the earth oven, after which quantities were dried and stored for winter. To prepare, the dried leaves were soaked to remove the bitter taste, and then boiled.

Common Monkey Flower *(Mimulus guttatus)* -- leaves boiled.

Musk-Plant *(Mimulus moschatus)* -- young plants boiled.

Miner's Lettuce *(Montia perfoliata)* -- stems, leaves and blossoms eaten raw.

Twiggy Water Dropwort *(Cenanthe)* -- stems eaten raw.

Sweet Cicely *(Osmorrhiza nuda)* -- leaves boiled.

Sheep Sorrel *(Rumex acetosella)* -- leaves pulverized, moistened with water, and eaten with salt. Sour, vinegary taste.

Green Dock *(Rumex conglomeratus)* -- leaves cooked and eaten as greens, but the seeds not used.

Tree Clover *(Trifolium ciliatum)* -- eaten raw or steamed, or dried and stored.

Cow Clover *(Trifolium involucratum)* -- eaten raw; never cooked or dried. This white-blossomed clover had a vinegar flavor.

Tomcat Clover *(Trifolium tridentatum)* -- eaten raw or steamed before it bloomed. Steamed leaves were spread out and dried in the sun for storage and winter use.

Mule-Ears *(Wyethia helenioides)*-- young shoots were eaten raw after peeling off the outer coating. Sweetish taste.

Manzanita berries were crushed by the Miwok to make a sweet, unfermented cider. To make this drink the berries were boiled briefly and then ground into a coarse meal. This was placed in a winnowing basket set over a watertight cooking basket. Water was then percolated over the meal until all the flavor was gone from it. The cider would keep for a couple of days before souring.

The Miwok, like other central Californians, did not consider berries and fruit as important food sources. Most were eaten raw, but Barrett and Gifford report three that sometimes were cooked:

California Laurel *(Umbellularia californica)* -- the fruit was roasted in ashes and eaten.

Blue Elderberry *(Sambucus glauca)* -- was cooked and then dried for winter consumption, occasionally being recooked in the winter.

Toyon *(Photinia arbutifolia)* -- the large red clusters of edible berries underwent protracted preparation as food. A preliminary boiling was followed by baking in a deep narrow earth oven. The berries were eaten with seed meal.

The acorn, the Miwok's staff of life, was harvested on the ground in late autumn and early winter. Acorns were hulled by standing them on end on a stone anvil and striking with a hammerstone. Only the acorn of the White or Valley Oak did not respond to this method of hulling because of a tendency to mash rather than crack open, and thus it was usually hulled by teeth.

Shelled acorn meats were pounded into meal by women who congregated at the bedrock mortars or, less frequently, at movable mortars. The meal was finely ground, sifted and leached of its tannin. This latter operation was done in a shallow basin scooped out of sandy soil. The meal was placed in this depression and water poured over it. About ten leachings were necessary, starting with cold water and progressing to very hot water. The meal was tasted and examined for whiteness, and when the Indian woman was satisfied all tannin had been removed, she scooped out the leached meal, removing what sand had clung to it.

The acorn meal was used in four ways:

Soup -- a large (thirty-quart) cooking basket was set on the ground, and into it was poured a concoction of two quarts of leached meal mixed with six or seven quarts of warm water. White hot stones were placed into the basket, causing the thin gruel to boil violently. More water and more hot

Captain McKinzie with bedrock mortars and stones near the Rich Gulch Hotel, Calaveras County. October, 1906.

stones were added, the cook stirring the gruel frequently to prevent the stones from burning through the basket.

When cooking was completed, the stones were lifted out, scraped of adhering meal, and dropped into cold water for final salvaging of the meal. From two quarts of meal the cook brought forth ten or twelve quarts of acorn soup.

Mush -- prepared the same as soup except that the whole was cooked to a thick glutinous state by increasing the ratio of meal to water.

Bread -- acorn meal dough was baked in the earth oven. Two kinds of bread -- black "leavened" and white "unleavened" -- were baked. The former, a dark brown color, was made from water oak acorns, "leavened" with a pinch of water oak bark ashes added to the dough.

Biscuits -- made of acorn mush. The hot mixture was dipped into small baskets which were then cooled for a short time in water. The cooling caused the ball of mush to loosen from the basket, and it could then be slid out into the water where it was left to thoroughly cool. Barrett and Gifford report that these biscuits, much used at feasts, had the consistency of a modern gelatin dessert.

The deer was the Miwok's most important source of meat. The hunter brought down game in five ways: By stretching a net over a deer trail during the September-October migration of animals from higher elevations to lower and the April-May migration from lower to higher elevations; by use of a deer trap; by driving the animals over a precipice; by getting close enough to the animals to shoot them with bow and arrow; or by running down an animal.

The deer trap was a V-shaped brush fence with snares set in openings at the angle of the V. Hunters would drive the deer into the V.

The Miwok hunter used several disguises to approach his prey, including deer masks and even the entire skin of a deer. Running down a deer usually took two days, but a fast runner could tire a deer in a day.

The deer was gutted where it was slain, but skinning usually took place at the hunter's home.

Barrett and Gifford recorded the usual method of distributing the meat:

"The stomach was given to a companion of the hunter, especially an older man. It was cooked at once for about two hours, covered with damp earth, ashes, coals, and on top of all a slow fire. In it were placed the cleaned entrails, windpipe, lights, and longitudinal pieces of flesh from near the kidneys. Blood also was added. After cooking, the stomach was tied in a bundle with willow or chaparral twigs and fastened to a stick, so that it might be carried over the shoulder.

"The liver was given to some old woman, such a one as had always given the hunter acorn mush when she made it. The liver was considered a delicacy. It was boiled in a basket. The hunter's mother-in-law and wife reserved the sirloin, which was cooked on the coals for them by the hunter, his mother, or his grandmother. It was not proper for his mother-in-law or wife to cook it. The cooking was done within the dwelling. If there were more people to eat the meat than there was room for, some were fed outdoors.

The forelegs and hind legs were given by the hunter to relatives and neighbors. The body was given to his wife's relatives (brother, father, etc.), also to son-in-law and daughter-in-law. The hunter ate but little himself. Being a good hunter, all brought him seed meal and he was plentifully supplied with that. Of course, a hunter had relatives by marriage and neighbors who reciprocated, so that he was usually amply supplied with venison. If a hunter kept what he killed he was looked down upon.

"When all men of the hamlet hunted, the kill was divided among them, regardless of whether some got deer or not. Meanwhile the women prepared acorns and other vegetable foods, and regaled the hunters with all sorts of delicacies."

The men also hunted elk and antelope in the lower elevations, more often than not in the territory of the Yokuts. The hunting parties were large -- perhaps a dozen or more men.

The mountain-dwelling Miwok (except those in the Central area) killed and ate bear. Again the hunting parties were large.

Rabbits were the next most important food animal after deer. These were caught with nets, often with an entire village participating in beating the brush and chasing the animals into the snare. In winter in the higher

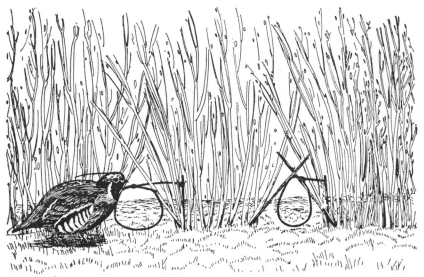

Brush fence snare.

elevations, hunters pursued and clubbed rabbits in the snow.

Beaver and squirrels were also hunted, principally with bow and arrow.

The quail was the Miwok's most important food bird. These he took by means of human hair snares set in small openings along a brush fence. Band-tailed pigeons were snared in fences built near springs.

The Miwok used a noose trap to capture pigeons, jays, red-shafted flickers and other birds. Of course, whenever the opportunity presented itself, hunters would shoot birds with arrows.

The Plains Miwok had access to and greater dependence on waterfowl and fish, especially salmon, than did their foothill cousins. What fish the latter caught they did so by means of seine, harpoon, spear or by hand. Mashed buckeye nuts and soaproot were put in small pools to poison fish, causing them to surface.

The Miwok also ate river mussels, fresh-water clams, and a variety of land snail.

Tobacco was the only plant the Miwok cultivated, but most of the supply came from wild plants. Planting was done in March, usually on a well-watered piece of ground, and always by old men. Tobacco was smoked in a short, tubular wooden pipe made of oak, ash, maple root or manzanita. The Central and Southern Miwok smoked a straight elder tube. Men and boys did the smoking. Women resorted to it only as a cure for bad colds.

When you were smoking and a friend came by, the sociable thing to do was to pass your pipe to him. After a few puffs, the friend would return the pipe and continue on his way.

The Miwok also used a concoction of powdered tobacco and water as an emetic. The Central and Southern Miwok ate a mixture of pulverized tobacco and lime as a purifier, particularly after a heavy meal. The tobacco thus taken induced vomiting, after which the overindulger washed himself and went to sleep.

To complete this picture of the Miwok's material world, we turn finally to medicines. Like all people in all times, including those reading these words, the Miwok depended a great deal on ritual and religion for the curing of sickness.

The Miwok shamans had in their kits a great many songs to combat the various human afflictions. They also practiced a ritualistic form of sucking out evil or causes of evil from their patients. For this work the doctor used a hollow wooden tube. Of course, all but the very young knew the doctors cleverly secreted the evil-causing object in his mouth before he pretended to suck it from an aching head or a sore shoulder or a cramping stomach -- but a good doctor could put on such a convincing show that when he finally reached into his mouth and produced the offensive pine needle, deer tooth, or dead lizard, the patient could not help but feel some relief.

Some illnesses required set ceremonials and dances. Scarification was still another means of making a sick person well.

Nearly all of these methods -- especially the ceremonials and dances --

Baited snare.

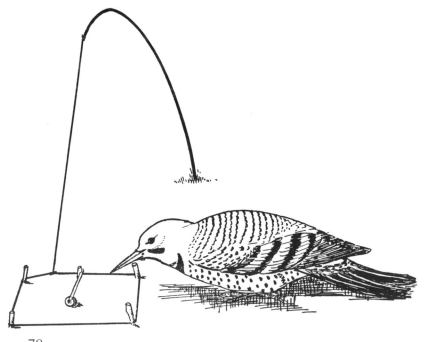

were practiced in conjunction with the taking of herb medicines. It is interesting to note that the Miwok list of medicinal plants overlaps by only about ten percent the plants used by Pomo, Yuki and Wailaki Indians. Some of the Miwok medicines (and the major decimating diseases) were introduced by Caucasians.

The list of medicinal plants compiled by Barrett and Gifford is a long one, and is reproduced here in condensed form. The maladies for which the medicine was taken follow the plant names:

Lowland Fir *(Abies grandis)* -- colds and rheumatism -- applied externally and internally.

Yarrow *(Achillaea millefolium)* -- bad colds, influenza -- leaves and flowers steeped and drunk or applied externally. Mashed leaves bound to wounds to stop pain.

Giant Hyssop *(Agastache urticifolia)* -- measles -- boiled and drunk. Also used as a cure for rheumatism.

Angelica *(Angelica breweri)* -- headache, cold -- root was chewed. Also was chewed and rubbed on the body to ward off snakes.

Dutchman's Pipe *(Aristolochia californica)* -- colds -- plant steeped and the decoction drunk.

Wormwood *(Artemisia vulgaris)* -- rheumatism -- decoction of the leaves was drunk. Wormwood had a variety of other uses: worn in the nostrils by mourners when crying; leaves inserted in one nostril for headache; leaves rubbed over the body to ward off ghosts; wormwood and other medicines were balled and attached to a necklace to prevent dreaming of the dead; corpse handlers rubbed themselves with wormwood to avoid being haunted by the ghost of the deceased.

Mugwort *(Artemisia vulgaris heterophylla)* -- used like wormwood.

Purple Milkweed *(Asclepias cordifolia)* -- root used as a general medicine.

Milkweed *(Asclepias speciosa)* -- veneral diseases -- a decoction of the root was taken in small doses. Milkweed milk also applied to warts.

Balsam Root *(Balsamorrhiza sagittata)* -- rheumatism, headache, other pain -- root was ground, boiled, cooled and drunk.

California Barberry *(Berberis pinnata)* -- heartburn, ague, consumption, rheumatism -- root decoction was drunk. For cuts, wounds and abrasions, a small piece of root was chewed and the resultant liquid placed in the injury. Warriors carried a piece of this root as first aid in battle.

Canchalagua *(Centaurium exaltatum)* -- toothache, stomach-ache, other internal pains, consumption -- decoction of stems and leaves was drunk.

Canchalagua *(Centaurium venustum)* -- pneumonia, fever, ague -- a decoction, made with brandy, of the flowers and leaves was drunk.

Mountain Misery *(Chamaebatia foliolosa)* -- rheumatism, diseases manifested by skin eruptions (chicken pox, measles, smallpox) -- leaves steeped in hot water and drunk hot. The skin eruption diseases were never treated by a shaman.

Mexican Tea *(Chenopodium ambrosiodes)* -- swelling, toothache, ulcerated tooth, gonorrhea, rheumatism -- plant was either boiled or used raw as a poultice.

Pipe-Stem *(Clematis lasiantha)* -- running sores, burns -- plant was burned and its charcoal pulverized and dusted on affected area.

Cypress *(Cupressus)* -- colds, rheumatism -- decoction of stems was drunk.

Durango Root *(Datisca glomerata)* -- sores, rheumatism -- root was pulverized and decoction was used as a wash.

Tolguacha *(Datura meteloides)* -- Shamans sometimes ate the root or drank a decoction of this plant to induce a delirium, during which they ran about wildly and saw strange visions.. Although the valley-dwelling Yokuts made general use of datura, the Miwok limited its use as described above.

Rattlesnake Weed *(Daucus pusillus)* -- snake bite -- plant was chewed and placed on the wound.

Scouring-Rush *(Equisetum)* -- stems used as a general medicine.

Fleabane *(Erigeron foliosus)* -- fever, ague -- a boiled and cooled decoction of the washed and pounded root was drunk. Fleabane was a trade item from the north.

Yerba Santa, Mountain Balm *(Eriodictyon californicum)* -- coughs, colds, stomach-ache, rheumatism -- leaves and flowers steeped in hot water and drunk. Sometimes the leaves were chewed, or warmed and used as a plaster on aching or sore spots.

Golden Yarrow *(Eriophyllum caespitosum)* -- aches -- leaves were bound over the sore place.

Rattlesnake Weed *(Euphorbia ocellata)* -- snake bite -- leaves were mashed and rubbed into the wound. A decoction was drunk as a blood purifier.

Thyme-Leaf Spurge *(Euphorbia serpyllifolia)* -- running sores -- decoction of the leaves used as a wash.

Sweet-Scented Bedstraw *(Galium triflorum)* -- dropsy -- boiled and drunk as a tea.

Incised Cranesbill *(Geranium incisum)* -- aching joints -- root was pulverized and steeped and then rubbed on joints.

California Everlasting *(Gnaphalium decurrens)* -- swelling -- pungent leaves of this plant were bound over the afflicted area.

Gum Plant *(Grindelia robusta)* -- running sores -- leaves were steeped and the decoction used as a wash.

Gold Fern *(Gymnogramma triangularis)* -- toothaches -- plant was chewed.

Tree Haplopappus *(Haplopappus)* -- stomach trouble, rheumatism -- boiled decoction of the leaves was drunk hot for stomach trouble; applied to rheumatic parts. Women sometimes drank this tea during menstruation and after childbirth, but it was too strong a remedy to be used during parturition. Leaves were applied to boils to bring them to a head. Also bound over sores on the feet.

Hedge-Leaved Haplopappus *(Haplopappus cuneatus)* -- colds -- decoction of the stems was drunk.

Tarweed *(Hemizonia virgata)* -- measles, general fevers -- a bath with a decoction of this plant was used.

Gold-Wire *(Hypericum concinnum)* -- running sores -- boiled, and used as a wash.

Cheese-Weed *(Malva parviflora)* -- running sores, boils, swelling -- leaves, soft stems and flowers were steeped and used as a poultice.

Spearmint *(Mentha spicata)* -- stomach trouble, diarrhea -- hot tea of the boiled leaves was drunk.

Buena Mujer *(Mentzelia)* -- pulverized seeds were mixed with water, or preferably fox or wildcat grease, and applied as a poultice.

Monkey Flower *(Mimulus)* -- diarrhea -- root used to make a tea with astringent properties.

Mustang Mint *(Monardella lanceolata)* -- colds, headaches -- decoction of the leaves, upper stems and flowers was drunk.

Mountain Pennyroyal *(Monardella odoratissima)* -- colds, fevers -- decoction of the stems and flower heads was drunk.

White Navarretia *(Navarretia cotulaefolia)* -- swelling -- boiled, and decoction applied externally.

Snake Root *(Osmorrhiza)* -- snake bite -- chewed and put on snake bite.

Bird's Foot Fern *(Pellaea ornithopus)* -- nose-bleed -- steeped in hot water and drunk. Also drunk as a spring medicine and blood purifier.

Small-Flowered Beard-Tongue *(Pentstemon breviflorus)* -- colds -- steeped and drunk.

Various-Leaved Bluebell *(Phacelia heterophylla)* -- fresh wounds -- plant was dried, pulverized and applied.

Horned Milkwort *(Polygala cornuta)* -- coughs, colds and pains -- diluted decoction was drunk. An undiluted decoction served as an emetic.

Knotweed, Alpine Smartweed *(Polygonum bistortoides)* -- sores, boils -- the root was mashed and used as a poultice.

Mountain Mint *(Pycnanthemum californicum)* -- colds -- boiled as a tea.

White Oak *(Quercus lobata)* -- running sores, sore umbilicus in babies -- outer bark pulverized and dusted over sore place. A bitter decoction was drunk as a cough medicine.

Interior Live Oak *(Quercus wislizenii)* -- same as White Oak.

Cascara *(Rhamnus rubra)* -- a decoction of the bark was drunk as a cathartic. It was the use of this bark by the California tribes which first brought this remedy to the attention of physicians, with the result that cascara is a familiar item in today's medicine cabinet.

Wild Rose *(Rosa californica)* -- pains, colic -- leaves and berries were steeped and drunk.

Green Dock *(Rumex conglomeratus)* -- boils -- root was pulverized, boiled, and the decoction was drunk and the boiled root applied externally.

Blue Elderberry *(Sambucus)* -- ague -- decoction made from the blossoms and drunk.

Poison Sanicle *(Sanicula bipinnata)* -- snake bite -- plant was boiled and applied to the bite.

Purple Sanicle *(Sanicula bipinnatifida)* -- A cure-all when the root was boiled and the decoction drunk.

Gamble Weed *(Sanicula menziesii)* -- snake bite, wounds -- pulverized leaves placed on wound.

Skullcap *(Scutellaria angustifolia)* -- sore eyes -- decoction used as a wash. Also drunk for coughs and colds.

Wild Rye *(Sitanion)* -- used dry or green by shaman to strike patient with, before and after sucking.

Black Nightshade *(Solanum nigrum)* -- sore eyes -- decoction used as a wash.

Common Goldenrod *(Solidago californica)* -- toothaches -- a small quantity of a decoction was held in the mouth.

Pitcher Sage *(Sphacele calycina)* -- fever, ague, headache -- decoction of the leaves was drunk.

Snowberry *(Symphoricarpos albus)* -- colds, stomach-ache -- root was pounded and steeped to make a decoction which was drunk.

Vinegar Weed, Camphor Weed *(Trichostema lanceolatum)* -- colds, malaria, headache, ague, general debility, stricture of the bladder -- decoction of the leaves and flowers was drunk. A bath with this decoction was a preventive measure against ague and smallpox. If the bath was not employed in time to prevent smallpox, then

81

the patient was bathed with a decoction made from the large, flat leaves of the incense cedar. This cured the pustules and prevented serious skin eruptions. With this was drunk a decoction of Fleabane. Many people were said to have been saved by this treatment during the epidemic of 1875. Sitting over a steaming decoction of the Vinegar Weed was a cure for uterine trouble, but was never used during pregnancy.

California Laurel *(Umbellularia californica)* -- headache -- leaves and twigs were bound on the forehead.

Nettle *(Urtica gracilis)* -- rheumatism -- decoction was made of the root and used as a bath. Powdered leaves were sometimes rubbed on the affected part and produced a fiery itching.

Mule Ears *(Wyethia angustifolia)* -- fever -- decoction of the leaves was used as a bath to produce a profuse perspiration.

Mexican Balsamea *(Zauschneria californica)* -- tuberculosis, kidney and bladder trouble -- decoction of the leaves was drunk.

In addition to the plants in this list, the Miwok had a number of unidentified plants that were used for remedies, including Mild Cucumber (venereal diseases), Sepesepa (stomach trouble), and Hokisa (a plant imported from the north which was smoked to keep the ghost away at a funeral).

The extent of this list is evidence that, contrary to some historians' assertion that the Indians were lazy and ignorant, the Miwok did the best they could to cure their ills. Any comparison of Miwok medicine with that of the white man must, to be fair, be made to the white man's medical practices of 150 years ago and not to our present knowledge in this field.

9

In Harmony With Earth

"Get up. Get up. Get up. Get up. Get up. Wake up. Wake up. Wake up. People get up on the south side, east side, east side, east side, east side, north side, north side, north side, lower side, lower side, lower side. You folks come here. Visitors are coming, visitors are coming. Strike out together. Hunt deer, squirrels. And you women strike out, gather wild onions, wild potatoes. Gather all you can. Gather all you can. Pound acorns, pound acorns, pound acorns. Cook, cook. Make some bread, make some bread. So we can eat, so we can eat, so we can eat. Put it up, and put it up, and put it up. Make acorn soup so that the people will eat it. There are many coming. Come here, come here, come here, come here. You have to be dry and hungry. Be for awhile. Got nothing here. People get up, people around get up. Wake up. Wake up so you can cook. Visitors are here now and all hungry. Get ready so we can feed them. Gather up, gather up, and bring it all in, so we can give it to them. Go ahead and eat. That's all we have. Don't talk about starvation, because we never have much. Eat acorns. There is nothing to it.

"Eat and eat. Eat. Eat. Eat. Eat. So that we can get ready to cry. Everybody get up. Everybody get up. All here, very sad occasion. All cry. All cry. Last time for you to be sad..."

This speech was delivered by Chief Yanapayak at Balk Rock in 1913 and recorded on the phonograph by University of California scientists.

It is an example of a summons to a mourning ceremony, delivered directly by the chief in small villages, and in larger villages by the chief's speaker.

The chief was the top man in the community, not only because of his hereditary prerogatives, but because he usually had more shell money, owned numerous dance costumes, and had other wealth.

The very powerful chief had two or three groups of young men, perhaps half a dozen to a group, who hunted and fished for him -- in order to supply food for communal fiestas, ceremonials and dances.

The big chief used his messenger to invite neighboring villagers to the function, and his speaker to address the assemblage. The latter's style of oratory is worth noting. He sat or kneeled on the ground and as he spoke

Miwok Indians on the Fremont Rancho near Mariposa.

he bowed so that his head almost touched the ground. To punctuate his speech, he swung his clenched fists horizontally in front of his stomach close to his body.

The preparation of deer was done at the chief's house by four ceremonial cooks. The meat was distributed to the homes of the villagers according to the instructions of the chief, who himself received the largest portion of meat.

The chiefs of larger villages did not participate in these hunts, and although they were head of the dancers and dance organizations, they usually did not dance.

When a chief died without a male heir, his daughter became chieftainess, to be succeeded by her son. If a dead chief's son was but a child, the boy's mother acted as regent until he was elevated to the chieftainship at about twenty years of age.

At the chief's death, the ceremonial house was burned, and in the case mentioned above the village would be without a place for ritual until the boy king was old enough to take over.

His ''coronation'' came with the building of a new ceremonial house and the renewal of village ceremonials.

84

Mrs. William Fuller, a Northern Miwok. Photo was taken in 1913.

Chief William Fuller.

The summons to the celebration was taken round to the neighboring villages by a messenger carrying a cord with four knots -- the significance being that in four days the fiesta begins. The next day one of the knots was removed and the people knew there were but three days to go.

The new ceremonial house was built under the direction of the village speaker. Such a speaker's instructions were recorded:

"That boy is getting to be a chief. Now all of you people get ready for him. Get everything ready. Be prepared to set up the poles and to fix the ceremonial house. The young chief is going to do the same as his father used to do. Now all of you men get ready.

"Put those poles up for him. All of you men get ready. Have the ceremonial house ready just the same as for his father. The young chief is going to do just the same as his father.

"He is going the same way as his father did. It is just the same, just the same. That is what his words tell us. All of you people get ready, for he is going to make a big celebration when the ceremonial house is completed.

"Listen, all of you women. All of you women get the pine needles, get the pine needles. He is going to do the same as his father did. He is going the same way as his father. He has thought of himself. He has thought of himself.

"He has prepared himself since his father died. He has prepared himself since his father died. He is going to do the same as his father. He has prepared himself since his father died. He has prepared himself since his father died. He is going to do the same as his father.

"He is going to do the same as his father. He is going to do things as his father did. Get the things ready. Get the things ready. Fix the ground. Make the ground level.

85

*Chief William Fuller, in spe[c]-
tacular headdress. Fuller was t[h]e
leader of the Miwok [in]
Tuolumne County.*

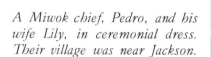

*A Miwok chief, Pedro, and his
wife Lily, in ceremonial dress.
Their village was near Jackson.*

"Get the poles. There are lots of poles around us; lots of poles around us. Get those poles which are nearest.

"He is all right; he is all right. He is becoming a chief just like his father. That is what you will do. That is what you will do when the big celebration comes. He is just the same. He is going to be just the same kind of man that his father was. There is nobody around us close by, so he is going to make the celebration himself. He is going to get ready.

"He is going to get ready for a big celebration after that ceremonial house is finished. Do not say 'I am not in it.' Do not say that. All of you people act the same as you used to. He is going to go just the same as his father and take care of us well.

"If you say that you are not like the old-people it will go different with you, it will go different. Things will turn out differently.

"We are going to do the same things that the old-people in the early days used to do, the people who told us what a real celebration was and what a real chief should be.

"We follow the customs of those ancient people, and we do what they used to do in the early days. We will try to do what they used to do, when the time comes, when the night comes. He is doing the same way.

"He is doing well. He is going to be a good chief. He is doing well.

"You can fix the ceremonial house and fix the ground for the ceremonial house. He is doing all right. He is doing all right. He is doing all right. I am glad he is going the right way.

"He is doing all right. Get the brush and the pine needles for the ceremonial house. Get those poles that go across the top, those that go across. Have the ceremonial house ready, so that we shall all be glad from now on.

"All of you people, I guess you have heard what I have said. Get ready. Get ready."

This speech, recorded by University of California anthropologists in the early part of this century, has two themes that give the Miwok away so far as his life pattern is concerned.

The first is the desire for continuance. Can one imagine a contemporary politician promising that he will be and do exactly as his predecessor? He may promise a return to the ''spirit'' of the days of Washington, Jefferson, Jackson and Lincoln, but he will likely add that he will be his ''own man''. Not so with the Miwok. No stirring promises; no brand new products; no blueprint for change. No ''new deal'' or ''new frontier''. Indeed, the Miwok emphasis is on return from inadvertent change.

The second Miwok thrust is to involve the entire community.

What the Miwok lacked by way of material security he made up for in psychological security. Participation in the sacred ritual which gently prodded and encouraged the good half of the universe, while neutralizing the evil half, was actual and physical. The Miwok sang sacred songs and danced sacred dances -- acts which stood between the naked man and the vastness of earth and sky and the tremendous forces contained therein.

The Miwok were not a ritual dominated people. Their daily or common practices to assure the well-being of the people and ward off doom were mild and hardly ominous.

The maiden, at her first menstruation, was confined, her diet restricted, and her chores limited.

Before eating certain foods, especially the first of the season, the Miwok performed ceremonies of ritualistic pressing, blowing and sucking of the prospective eaters.

Certain seeds were strewn on the Ceremonial House prior to sacred dances.

Fathers practiced a form of semi-couvade during the birth of children. They remained quietly indoors and did not hunt, fish, gamble or mingle with the people.

To understand why the Miwok did and said certain things, we must understand his view of life. In large measure, this system of belief was common to all American Indians.

These convictions, too deep-seated for articulation by the Miwok, consisted of four tenets:

First -- Life is very dangerous. White men know this too, but they are not preoccupied with the realization.

Second -- Nature is more powerful than man. Any attempt to master

Close-up of a feather dance skirt photographed in 1909, at West Point, Calaveras County.

Feather dance plumes.

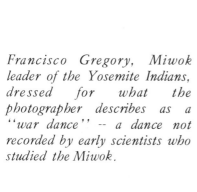

Francisco Gregory, Miwok leader of the Yosemite Indians, dressed for what the photographer describes as a "war dance" -- a dance not recorded by early scientists who studied the Miwok.

nature is futile. The thing to do in order to get along with nature is to behave properly and perform the proper rituals.

Third -- Human nature is neither good nor evil -- both qualities are blended in the whole person. Further, one cannot separate the person's mind from his body.

Fourth -- This life is all that counts. It is not a preparation for another life, although the possibility of an after-life is not dismissed.

The Central California Indian's concept of the origin of the world is not far from the plan of Genesis. They say a primeval ocean preceded the true creation. Their creator had a brother who helped with the work, but he tended to be a bungler, hence this imperfect world and the co-existence of evil with good.

Coyote, a marplot, later took the place of the creator's brother in Miwok mythology. It was sticks of clay in Coyote's house that became men and women.

Four is the Miwok sacred number. His ritual is repetitive, usually performed four times; the dance stage contains four parts; a dancer passes a piece of regalia over his head four times before putting it on; ritual acts are performed four times consecutively; each dance is in four parts; the ceremonies last four days.

The Miwok borrowed his basic ritual system from the Sacramento

Valley area where the Kuksu religion flourished. The Kuksuyu was the most sacred and elaborate of the Miwok ceremonies. It was powerful medicine. There was danger to performer and audience in a misstep. The Kuksuyu dancer, one of three characters in the ceremony, wore a raven feather-covered cloak which concealed his entire body. A hawk-wing headdress completed what had to be the most spectacular Miwok physical creation. These costumes were destroyed at the death of a Kuksuyu dancer.

The Kuksuyu impersonator and a second character, Mochilbe, were always men. The third dancer, Osabe ("woman"), could be man or woman. If a man, a waist-length wig was used.

All Miwok sacred dances were impersonations of supernatural beings, and while anthropologists have recorded every detail of these dances, practically nothing is known of the beings central to the ritual. In short, we know how they danced, but not why. "Tom Williams (a Miwok informant) thinks that the Kuksuyu is a sulesko, a sort of spirit," is the sum of Kuksuyu substance that we get from the anthropological records of Central Miwok ceremonies compiled by E. W. Gifford.

Children were allowed to witness the dances that took place in the ceremonial house. Regarding the Kuksuyu, they were repeatedly reminded of the sacredness of the dance and warned not to let a feather of the costume brush up against them for fear of its causing illness.

There are only two other Miwok dances, besides the Kuksuyu, in which the performers wore masks or hoods. These were the Helekasi and Sulesko, in which the dancers completely enveloped their heads in deerskin hoods. Paint and feathers were used in other dances to conceal the identity of the performer.

In some Miwok ritual, the dancers mimicked the antics of animals. Others employed clowns to keep things moving along. The Sulesko was a dance designed to cure people made ill from the ghosts of dead people.

The Miwok also had several profane or common dances which were performed purely for entertainment. Unlike the sacred dances, these held no element of danger for either performers or viewers.

During a four-day fiesta, several sacred and profane dances were given. In between performances, the townspeople and their guests ate, visited, slept, competed in sports contests, and above all gambled. The big fiestas came at auspicious times of the year -- at the start of hunting and fishing seasons and at the acorn harvest.

"There are six women and six men dancers. All the people would come into the roundhouse to watch them dancing.

"The chief would call, would have them come, telling them to watch the performance of the dancers, the singers, and those who would presently play the drum and the rattles.

"There were four singers. The women who were dancing would decorate themselves with feathers on their heads. They would dance until morning. When they stopped dancing in the morning they would leave, they would go to bathe in the creek.

"They would have Big Times in the roundhouse. They would eat acorn soup and acorn bread and ground squirrel meat, and wild cabbage and deer meat. The women, the men, the little children, they all used to come inside the roundhouse.

"They used to divide up the acorn soup and deer meat, and after they had divided it they would eat it with squirrel meat and cabbage, all of them together.

"Any ones who wanted would challenge each other. One would stake his bead belt, they would meet it with a belt of abalone shell. They would take the bones, and fix counting sticks, and then they would play hand games against each other. The people of the water moiety would gamble against those of the land moiety."

While the shaman took part in some dances, or coincidentally could have been a leading local performer in certain dances, his role as shaman was non-ceremonial. The shaman was a doctor, not a priest, and yet it has never been an easy matter to separate the two aspects of the healer, and especially among a people who did not separate soul from body. The parallel exists in modern society. There are some priests who are more doctor than priest; and some doctors who are more priest than doctor.

There were many kinds of shamans, for there were many sources of power in the Miwok's natural world. The more common practitioners were bear shaman, coyote shaman, rattlesnake shaman, salmon shaman, deer shaman, condor shaman and poison shaman.

The shaman's knowledge, skills and power were learned from an experienced shaman, perhaps an older relative, after the apprentice had received from nature an irrefutable calling to his vocation.

This summons came in many forms. Perhaps dreams of rushing water, or an encounter with a bear in the forest, or a miraculous recovery from eating a poison mushroom would be the determining factor in setting a young man on the path to becoming, respectively, a salmon, bear or poison shaman.

How does one teach the art of poisoning to a potential poisoner?

Here is a free translation of a Miwok lesson in poisoning:

"A man's father, when he begins to make him a poison shaman, places a crystal on the left hand of his son. After placing it there, he makes him eat the root of a plant with poisonous properties. The father takes his son into the brush. He does not eat anything for a day. He gives him porcupine quills, and he sticks a feather into the ground at a distance.

" 'Hit that!' he says, 'Hit that!' giving him the porcupine quills.

"He shoots the feather with the porcupine quills. Then he scatters earth upon it, and he calls the feather by name, as he scatters earth upon it...

"A man who is a poisoner must live far away from everyone. He must go out there near the place where he is living, and when he gets there he rolls a log about.

"He shouts, he hates to let his poison go. The poison is like fire. He calls the name of the one he is poisoning. He commands the poison, 'Go to his head!' he says.

91

Sometimes he says, 'Go to his breast!'

"To whatever place is mentioned, there goes the poison.

"After poisoning and killing someone, he cries for the man more than anyone. He grieves for the one he kills."

The shaman, of course, spent more time healing than killing -- but the latter is certainly a reasonable service to perform, or attempt to perform. It goes without saying that one cannot actually poison another person by shouting out the victim's name and commanding the poison to seek this particular mark; what one does, of course, is make the patient bent on obtaining revenge feel better in knowing that at least something is being done to secure the needed release.

If a Miwok village was large enough to have a chief and a ceremonial assembly house, then it also had a funeral fire tender whose job it was to cremate the dead. However, cremation was not universally practiced by the Miwok, although it was more prevalent than burial.

The fire tender took possession of the body immediately following death. It was his first function to watch over the corpse during the laying-in period in either a dwelling or the ceremonial house.

Meanwhile, word of the death was rapidly spread by the chief's messengers, who also advised of the funeral date -- almost invariably four days after death. (Sometimes, however, the chief would declare "one day is called four" and the deceased would be cremated or buried on the same day of his death. When this happened, feasting and merrymaking usually followed.)

The fire tender led the wailing for the deceased -- sometimes even before actual death. The practice was for the wailers, wearing pungent mugwort leaves in their nostrils, to walk or dance counterclockwise around the body. The fire tender also had the prerogative of suggesting that the funeral oration, delivered by the village speaker and others, begin.

When the addresses were concluded, the body was burned on a five-foot high pyre. The fire tender stayed by his fire until it was completely consumed, using a long pole to facilitate the burning.

Four days after the cremation, the dead man's personal property and house were burned.

A funeral for a chief or other important personage, such as a dancer, clown, singer, drummer or certain shamen, included a Hohi dance, which took the place of the usual wailing and dancing. Four singers and six male and four to six female dancers conducted the ceremony. The women dancers each carried a possession of the deceased. The dance was divided into four parts, and during the rest periods the mourners conducted themselves as they would at an ordinary funeral. That is, they commenced to wail and stamp their feet or dance around the body.

A widow or widower did not attend the funeral. She or he was confined

DIGGER INDIANS OF CALIFORNIA BURNING THEIR DEAD

One of the few California Indian rites generally seen by outsiders was the cremation of the dead -- hence its relatively wide coverage in the press. Note group of observers at right, including two Chinese. This sketch by Mrs. C. Taylor appeared in Ballous Pictorial *for May 2, 1857. While all California Indians were labeled "Diggers", Mrs. Taylor's subjects are probably Southern Maidu in the vicinity of Placerville. The accompanying article stated the "Diggers" were probably the most "filthy, stupid and depraved" of all the Western Indians -- misinformation quoted from E. S. Capron's* History of California.

in a neighboring house -- actually locked in by an in-law. There the surviving partner's hair was singed, and worn short until death or remarriage.

The bereaved partner was confined for two months, during which time only vegetable food was eaten. He was allowed out of the house only at night.

The Miwok held a mourning ceremony about a year after a death. This was called a Yame, or "cry", and lasted four days, with the usual eating, visiting, sleeping and gambling. The Yame itself consisted of hour-long periods of wailing. After it was over the mourners were ceremonially washed by people of the opposite moiety.

Miwok death figures in legend and fact concerning the huge limestone caverns in the western foothills of the Sierra Nevada, particularly Moaning Cave two miles south of Vallecito in Calaveras County. Authoritative reports indicate there is more legend than fact in these stories.

Moaning Cave is a vertical limestone fissure more than 250 feet in depth. Archeologists have found human bones and artifacts on the floor of the main chamber, 180 feet below the cave mouth.

From the early 1850's reports of the cavern's human fossils have made their way into the press. San Francisco's *Daily Alta California* on November 6, 1853, told its readers that the cave contained "...a large number of human bones..." including "...some heads which were more or less petrified. Some of these latter were so fixed in the stone that the discoverers could not get them unbroken. Others, however, they obtained entire skeletons besides a number of bones. The party filled several sacks with earth and made their way back to the open air...They name their discovery the 'cave of the sepulchre'..."

In the same issue of the *Daily Alta California,* the editor gives a first-hand report of his examination of the crania: "...there is no petrification; there is a simple deposit of sulphate of lime...there being a continual drip from the roof above. There are about sixty-five skulls in all, many of which were so deep in the deposit that they could not be obtained without being broken to pieces...One of the skulls is covered by eight visibly distinct layers; and the *cicerone* informed us that probably a century was required to form each layer."

The editor ends with this remarkable observation: "The skulls are undoubtedly of Indians who lived long since. The cranial developments are very similar to those of the present Indians, though one of the skulls appear to have a very intellectual character."

None of the foothill caves have been used in recent times as tombs. Such caves were probably the home of Yayali, the legendary giant who searched the countryside for people to eat.

It was Yayali who killed Chipmunk and married his widow, and although Chipmunk's brother was able to trick Yayali and kill him in turn, still Miwok tradition holds that deep caverns such as Moaning Cave and Mercer's Caverns near Murphys are the homes of monsters. The more recent Indians would not have dreamed of throwing corpses of their tribesmen into the depths of these caves to be eaten.

10

Yosemite

Bancroft called Yosemite a "stronghold". To this beautiful and isolated Sierra Nevada valley, he reported, the Indians retreated after "committing their depredations upon white settlers".

When the white men discovered Yosemite, Bancroft continued, the "Indians became disheartened". Later they renewed their depredations, but finally retreated across the Sierra to the land of the Monos. Upon leaving these folks, the Yosemite Indians helped themselves to a few Mono cattle. The Monos followed and nearly exterminated the Yosemite warriors, leaving scarcely half a dozen alive. All women and children were carried off. But, the historian concludes, the Indians left as their legacy a name for every cliff and waterfall in the valley.

They also left the only authentic Miwok hero of whom we have any knowledge today, Chief Tenaya.

The story of Tenaya is rigidly documented in white literature, and we shall retell it here. But first we should listen to a Miwok informant, Chris Brown, who gives us a flavor of the man and his times:

"Long ago they say Tenaya talked about this, when the white people pushed him. He arrived somewhere, he went to Tenaya Lake and coming back he arrived.

"The white soldier found him, clubbed him and nearly killed him. They brought him this way, they took him to the west, to what the white men call Oakhurst. Who knows the Indian name?

"There they had nothing to eat for several days. They just lay there. They cracked acorns. After they got the acorns, they ate them. The meat and things that the white people gave them they threw away.

" 'They are killing us,' they said. They took Tenaya himself to the San Joaquin Valley. Then at night he felt sorry for himself. The soldier killed his child. 'I'm thinking about my child, about going back to him, to see him and take care of him,' he said. Then at night he told the Indians, 'It is said that if we don't go with these white people they will kill us and get rid of all of us. All of you go with these white people, but I am going to take care of my child, to see how he is there. I am going to bury him and burn him,' he said. He ran from there this way.

"Lebrado, or somebody, maybe he, he was a little boy, he talked to me and told me that in answer, he told me at night. He came along the creek, they waded the creek this way. Everybody came. The soldiers got there the next day, the Indians had gone and run away.

''But the soldier thinks, 'They are tired, let them rest. They have nothing to eat,' he said. 'They won't go anywhere,' said he, this one, what was his name, his captain. Then they came this way. They went along the creek, they climbed up to what they now call Bridal Veil. Then below he reached where the bear ate his child, dragging him around. 'He didn't keep very well,' he thought. He took his child and brought him to Bear Creek, as they call it, and buried it there, his bones. He himself died too, he was killed on the other side of the mountain by the Monos.

''They clubbed him. After they clubbed him and killed him they laid him out. John Hutchins, whom we call Tom Hutchins, he brought him, nothing but his hair, he brought it to the Indians. The Indians wept, they cried all one night. The next day they buried him there in Yosemite, at what is called the Museum. He was buried there, his dust, as they say. Then the Indians, 'They are different, they are another kind of people, it is said,' they thought. 'That's right,' they said.''

Yosemite was a summer resort for Miwok as well as other Indians in the vicinity.

The white man discovered the beautiful valley on what we would call today a ''search and destroy'' mission. The Indians had retaliated against the serious disruption of their way of life by striking at the white trading posts and settlements below Yosemite.

All of the Indians in the general vicinity except those secreted in Yosemite Valley were either killed or captured by the white militia. Six ''tribes'' signed a treaty with the Commissioners on March 19, 1851, which, along with similar treaties mentioned earlier, the U. S. Senate never ratified and kept secret for decades because of pressure exerted from the mining- and land-interest dominated California legislature.

The treaty granted the six Indian groups a reservation between the Merced and Tuolumne rivers, near the division line between Yokuts and Miwok in that region. While most of the five hundred or so Indians who settled here were Yokuts, no doubt a considerable number were Miwok.

The terms were these: the Indians acknowledged U.S. jurisdiction and gave up all rights to lands in California outside of reservation lands. The U.S., in turn, agreed to protect the Indians and teach them useful arts. The government also said it would give the six ''tribes'' jointly a hundred head of beef and a hundred sacks of flour a year -- not for perpetuity (that sort of miscalculation had been made on the Plains and was not to be repeated in California), but for two years, 1851 and 1852.

In 1853 Lt. Edward Beale, California Superintendent of Indian Affairs, presented evidence that one of the treaty-making commissioners had been involved in a dishonest contract, and that one contractor had taken for himself upwards to one-half of the cattle due the Indians.

By 1857 the Indian population on the reservation off of the Merced River had dwindled to eighty souls. The sub-Indian Agent reported that the Indians there ''have been forced, to some extent, into peddling their women to subsist''.

A Miwok Indian baby in a papoose carrier. Yosemite Valley, 1934.

This is the reservation the government gave to the Indians in exchange for Yosemite and its environs. Tenaya met with representatives of the commission in March, 1851, and agreed to bring out the Indians still at large in the valley. The chief led seventy-two of the estimated band of two hundred tribesmen into captivity at the Fresno reservation. But a people used to centuries of mountain freedom found the white man's camp a living death, and Tenaya's people escaped.

In May of that year, the militia mounted a second expedition and in the ensuing battle, Tenaya was captured and his youngest son slain. The next month the captured Yosemites arrived for the second time in Fresno.

"My people do not want anything from the Great Father you tell us about," Tenaya said. "The Great Spirit is our Father and he has supplied us with all we need. We do not want anything from white men. Let us

97

remain in the mountains where we were born, where the ashes of our fathers have been given to the winds."

Such eloquence gives testimony both to Tenaya's abilities as a leader and to the humanness of the people he led. Apparently it had its effects on the authorities, for the chief and his family were allowed to return to Yosemite.

In May, 1852, two prospectors were killed in Yosemite. Indians were blamed, and five of them were captured and executed on the spot.

Tenaya, knowing the whites would never consider five Indian lives sufficient payment for two white lives, led his people over the mountains to the Monos.

In the autumn of 1853 the Yosemites returned. By now it was clear to these people that it was safer to raid their allies than their enemies, and so they stole some Mono livestock -- an unspeakable breach of hospitality for which Tenaya and most of his tribesmen died.

The Miwok rank third among California Indians as suppliers of place names in the state. The Shoshoneans lead with thirty-three place names; the Chumash have twenty-eight; the Miwok -- including the Coast and Lake branches -- twenty-six.

The Miwok names for Yosemite landmarks are words used by tens of thousands of people each year.

Ahwahnee was the Southern Miwok name for the largest village in Yosemite Valley, and the Indians' name for the valley itself. The present Ahwahnee, which the Indians called "Wasama", is located forty miles from the Miwok's original Awani.

Yosemite itself is the Miwok word for "grizzly bear", or "killer". The Indian pronunciation, according to Kroeber, was "uzumati" or "uzhumati", the "u" spoken with rounded lips.

Hunto Mountain in the national park is from the Miwok word for "eye".

Pohono Falls in Yosemite is probably not a Miwok word, but is derived from "Pohonichi", the Yokuts' name for a Miwok group in the vicinity.

The South Dome is known by its Miwok name, Tissaack, the woman who, Indian tradition said, was transformed into a mountain.

Stephen Powers wrote in his *Tribes of California,* published in 1877, that Indian names had "effected such slight lodgment in our atlases" in other parts of the state that it was not worthwhile to attempt to set them right. But in Yosemite so many of the native names were preserved that we were faced with a different situation.

Popular guide books of the day stated that they had derived their catalogs of Indian names from white men.

"The Indians certainly have a right to be heard in this department at least," wrote Powers. "And when they differ from the interpreters every

A Miwok woman in Yosemite Valley, from the Hutchings collection.

right-thinking man will accept the statement of an intelligent aborigine as against a score of Americans.''

If the Miwoks of Yosemite did not know the simple words and place names of his own language, Powers was saying, then who in heaven's name did?

Powers hired a Miwok Choko (''dog'') named Old Jim to guide him around the valley to record the Miwok names of places. Here is Old Jim's list, and Powers' comments:

''Wa-kal'-la (the river). Merced River.

''Kai-al'-a-wa, Kai-al-au'-wa, the mountain just west of El Capitan.

''Put-put-on, the little stream first crossed on entering the valley on the north side.

''Lung-u-tu-ku-ya, Ribbon Fall.

''Po-ho-no, Bridal-Veil Fall. In Hutchings' Guide-Book, it is stated that the Indians believe this stream and the lake from which it flows to be bewitched, and that they never pass it without a feeling of distress and terror. Probably the Americans have laughed them out of this superstition, as it certainly is not now perceptible. This word is said to signify 'evil wind'. The only 'evil wind' that an Indian knows of is a whirlwind, which is 'poi-i-cha' or 'kan-u-ma'.

"Tu-tok-a-nu-la, El Capitan. This name is a permutative substantive formed from the verb 'tul-tak-a-na', to creep or advance by degrees, like a measuring-worm. This may, therefore, be called the 'Measuring-worm Stone'. (El Capitan was a very small rock. Bear and her two cubs lay down on it and went to sleep. In the morning they found themselves in a strange place for El Capitan had grown. It reached into heaven, and scraped past Moon. Everyone was crying in the valley because of the plight of the three bears. They decided that some one should climb El Capitan and bring them down. Mouse tried, but he only managed to climb a handbreadth and then fall down. Rat tried, but he too failed, climbing very little farther than Mouse. Raccoon and Grizzly Bear both failed. Mountain Lion tried, but he too failed. Then Measuring Worm came along. Insignificant and small as he was, he began climbing the rock step by step, a little at a time. A whole winter passed and still he climbed. Soon he disappeared from sight, and at last reached the top. There he found Bear and her two cubs had starved to death. Measuring Worm gathered their bones and brought them down and the people burned them in the usual way.)

"Ko-su-ko, Cathedral Rock.

"Pu-si-na, Chuk-ka (the squirrel and the acorn cache), a tall, sharp needle, with a smaller one at its base, just east of Cathedral Rock. Pu-si-na is squirrel, and chuk-ka is acorn-cache. A single glance at it will show how easily the simple savages, as they were pointing out to one another the various objects, imagined here a squirrel nibbling at the base of an acorn granary.

"Kom-pom-pe-sa, a low rock next west of Three Brothers. This is erroneously spelled Pompompasus, applied to Three Brothers, and interpreted 'mountains playing leap-frog'. The Indians know neither the word nor the game.

"Loi-a, Sentinel Rock.

"Sak-ka-du-eh, Sentinel Dome.

"Cho-lok (the fall), Yosemite Fall. This is the generic word for 'fall'.

"Um-mo-so (generally contracted by the Indians to Um-moas or Um-mo), the bold, towering cliff east of Yosemite Fall. According to Choko, there was formerly a hunting-station near this point, back in the mountains, where the Indians secreted themselves to kill deer when driven past by others. If we may credit him, they missed more than they hit. In his jargon of English, Spanish, and Indian, supplemented with copious and expressive pantomime, he described how they hid themselves in the booth, and how the deer came scurrying past; then he quickly caught up his bow and shot, shot, shot; then peered out of the bushes, looked blank, laughed, and cried out, 'All run away; no shoot um deer!'

"Ma-ta (the canyon), Indian Canyon. A generic word, in explaining which the Indians hold up both hands to denote perpendicular walls.

"Ham-mo-ko (usually contracted to Ham-moak), a generic word, used several times in the valley to denote the broken debris lying at the foot of the walls.

"U-zu-mai-ti La-wa-tuh (grizzly-bear skin), Glacier Rock. The Indians give it this name from the grayish, grizzled appearance of the wall and a fancied resemblance to a bear-skin stretched out on one of its faces.

"Tu-tu-lu-wi-sak, Tu-tul-wi-ak, the southern wall of South Canyon.

"Cho-ko-nip-o-deh (baby basket), Royal Arches. This curved and overhanging canopy-rock bears no little resemblance to an Indian baby-basket. Another form is cho-ko-ni; and either one means literally 'dog-place' or 'dog-house'.

"Tol-leh, the soil or surface of the valley wherever not occupied by a village; the commons. It also denotes the bank of a river.

"Pai-wai-ak (white water?), Vernal Fall. The common word for water is kik-kuh, but a-wai-a means a lake or body of water. I have detected a conjectural root, pai, pi, denoting white, in two languages.

"Yo-wai-yi, Nevada Fall. In this word also we detect the root of awaia.

"Tis-se-yak, South Dome. This is the name of a woman who figures in a legend....
the Indian woman cuts her hair straight across the forehead, and allows the sides to drop along her cheeks, presenting a square face, which the Indians account the acme of female beauty; and they think they discovered this square face in the vast front of South Dome.

"To-ko-ye, North Dome...

"Shun-ta, Hun-ta (the eye), the Watching Eye.

"A-wai-a (a lake), Mirror Lake.

"Sa-wah (a gap), a name occurring frequently.

"Wa-ha-ka, a village which stood at the base of Three Brothers; also, that rock itself. This was the westernmost village in the valley, and the next one above was:

"Sak-ka-ya, on the south bank of the river, a little west of Sentinel Rock. The only other village on the south bank was:

"Hok-ok-wi-dok, which stood very nearly where Hutching's Hotel now stands, opposite Yosemite Fall.

"A-wa-ni, a large village standing directly at the foot of Yosemite Fall. This was the ruling town, the metropolis of this little mountain democracy, and the giver of its name, and it is said to have been the residence of the celebrated chief Ten-ai-ya.

"Thus it will be seen that there were nine villages in Yosemite Valley, and, according to Choko, there were formerly others extending as far down as Bridal-Veil Fall, which were destroyed in wars that occurred before the whites came. At a low estimate these nine villages must have contained 450 inhabitants. Dr. L. H. Bunnell indirectly states that the valley was not occupied during the winter, and was used only as a summer resort and as a a place of refuge in case of defeat elsewhere; but the Indians now living say it was occupied every winter. This is quite possible, for Mr. Hutchings and others tarry there throughout the year without inconvenience. Moreover, the assertion of the Indians is borne out by the locations of the villages themselves, which Choko pointed out with great minuteness. With the exception of the two on the south bank they were all built as close to the north wall as the avalanches of snow and ice would permit, in order to get the benefit of sunshine, just as Mr. Hutchings's winter cottage is today. If they had been intended only for summer occupation they would have been placed, according to Indian custom, close to the river. And the fact that the Indians all leave the valley in the winter nowadays makes nothing against this theory, for they have become so dependent on the whites for the means of making a livelihood that they would go near to perish if they remained."

Much of the credit for the balance and sensibility of Yosemite placenames goes to one Lafayette Houghton Bunnell, known as "Doc" because of a bit of medical training.

Doc Bunnell accompanied the 1851 militia into Yosemite as an interpreter (in case Spanish-speaking mission renegades were encountered). But more than linguist and medicine man, he was a reader of poetry and a true lover of nature.

When the party he was with stumbled upon the beauty of the Yosemite chasm, Doc Bunnell knew the full scope of the opportunity that fate had thrust in the hands of the roughneck crew he was part of: it was in their power to name the marvels at their feet.

After descending to the valley floor and making camp, Doc Bunnell planted the idea of naming the place.

"The coarse jokes of the careless, and the indifference of the practical, sensibly jarred my more devout feelings," Bunnell wrote.

But the beauty of Yosemite came to Bunnell's aid. The men, mostly Texans with reputations to uphold, had been touched by what they had seen.

Names were suggested -- some foreign, some Biblical. Bunnell proposed the logic of an American name, and then, after that had settled into his listeners, the further logic -- and justice -- of an Indian name. The Texans listened.

The only local Indian name was that of the people they were pursuing -- the Yo-sem-i-ty.

Someone objected: "Devil take the Indians and their names! Why should we honor these vagabond murderers by perpetuating their name?"

"Damn the Indians and their names," cried another. "Let's call this 'Paradise Valley'."

Someone called for a vote. It was Paradise Valley versus Yo-sem-i-ty.

Modestly, Doc Bunnell describes the fateful election: "The question of giving the name of Yo-sem-i-ty was then explained; and upon a *viva voce* vote being taken, it was almost unanimously adopted."

Many placenames were given to Yosemite natural features in this and a subsequent visit to the valley by the militiamen. Doc Bunnell labored mightily to prevent sacrilege.

"Giant's Pillar", "Sam Patch's Falls", "Devil's Night-Cap", "Cloud's Rest", "Three Brother's Peak" (where three Indian brothers were captured), "Indian Creek" and other names were given -- and some were changed or abandoned through Doc Bunnell's efforts.

He sought out the Indian names for landmarks, lobbied for some, wisely rejected others ("Py-we-ack", "Yo-wy-we") as "ridiculous in sound".

Bunnell eliminated the obscene: "They were called by the Indians 'Kom-po-pai-qes' (the original name of the 'Three Brothers'), from a fancied resemblance of the peaks to the heads of frogs when sitting up ready to leap. A fanciful interpretation has been given the Indian name as meaning 'mountains playing leap-frog', but a literal translation is not desirable."

Bunnell is credited with naming Vernal Fall (the spray gave the effect of spring flowers). He changed "Yo-wy-we" to Nevada Fall. He accepted a friend's suggestion for the name Bridal Veil Fall. He used the Spanish for 'the captain' and it became El Capitan.

Doc Bunnell deserves a great deal of credit for his name-giving work. He was neither crude nor overly sentimental. He was, in a word, sincere -- and the placenames he was responsible for reflect this sincerity.

How was this valley created? The Miwok say it all started with a family quarrel! Half Dome had a spat with her husband, Washington Tower, and ran away into the Sierra. As she proceeded, she created the upper course of the Merced River and Yosemite Valley itself. From the burden basket she carried spilled the seeds which led to the Valley's luxuriant vegetable growth.

Washington Tower caught up with his wife and beat her severely. A globose basket she was carrying was flung to the north side of the canyon where it landed bottom upward to become North Dome.

Half Dome also had with her a baby cradle. This was thrown against the north wall of the canyon, where it became the Royal Arches.

As Half Dome received her punishment she wept bitterly and was transformed into the present great peak. Her tears stained the face of the monolith where they can be seen today as dark-streaked stains.

Washington Tower, having spent his wrath, went over to the north side of the Valley where he became a great shaft of granite.

Miwok legend parts the curtain of time and we glimpse a world far removed from the one we live in today. ''A long time ago there used to be a village near the foot of Yosemite Falls,'' begins a Miwok story recorded by Edward Gifford and Gwendoline Block in their 1930 book, *California Night Entertainments.* ''One day, a maiden from this village went to the stream for a basket of water. When she dipped her basket into the stream she brought it up full of snakes, instead of water as usual. So she went a little bit farther upstream and dipped her basket again. Again she brought it up full of snakes. Each time she went a little higher upstream and each time her basket filled with snakes.

''Soon she reached the fast-rushing waters at the foot of Yosemite Falls, and then suddenly a violent wind blew her into it. While being tossed around in the pool she gave birth to a child.''

The supernatural baby was covered with a blanket and taken to the village. When the mother took off the blanket ''immediately a violent gale arose and blew the entire village and people into the same pool the girl had been blown into. Nothing has ever been seen or heard of them since.

''The Poloti, a group of dangerous spirit women, live in the Yosemite Falls. It is believed these spirits were the cause of the disappearance of the village.''

Creating a world is beyond man's capacity both to do and to understand. The Miwok did not attempt either. Instead, they lived in the earth as they found it. Yosemite and the Sierra Nevada was their home. To their everlasting credit they left the land as they found it.

11

The People Today

A century and a quarter after their armed conquest, the Miwok show symptoms of reversing the downward slide toward oblivion.

The impact of the white man's sledgehammer stampede into Miwok lands in the 1850's reduced the Indians' numbers by perhaps seventy to eighty percent -- this in the span of a single generation!

Such a conquest, followed by generations of economic and social inferiority, can have but one effect: cultural trauma.

All people who suffer a brutal conquest -- whether Miwok or Mayan or Bushman or Negro or Jew or Roman-era Christian -- exhibit universal characteristics.

The first thing they attempt to do is isolate themselves from their conquerors -- physically, whenever possible; psychologically, when physical isolation is not possible.

Conquered people have, from the beginning of time, exhibited styles of behavior that their conquerors point to as *prima facie* evidence of the superiority -- the divine right, if you will -- of the conqueror over the conquered.

Over and over we hear the liturgy: these people (if the speaker admits that people is what they deserve to be called) are apathetic, withdrawn, irresponsible, lazy, poor managers, excessively factionalistic. They are shy. They are brutish. They are stupid. Add it all together and it comes out: we are, by comparison, wonderful.

A Northern California Indian reported at a recent All-Indian Conference on Education that young Indian children are getting more than entertainment from their television sets:

"I don't want to be an Indian anymore," a kindergartener told his aunt. When she asked why, he replied, "Because they are all bad, and I don't want to be one!"

In the Miwok Rancheria two miles north of Tuolumne City, the past is not remote. One hundred twenty years could be 120 months or 120 weeks or days, if one can command the eye to ignore the junked cars in the front yards of rude rural homes.

The round-house wears neat shakes and nearby is a tin-plated soft-drink stand that does some business during special occasions such as the Acorn Harvest Day celebration in September. An area newspaper ballyhooed this annual event with these words: "...the sands of time will be pushed back to before the arrival of the paleface in the New World as Indians from throughout the state will be outfitted in the colorful dress of their forefathers...Tons of acorns will be consumed in the form of tasty soup and bread just as the Indians did before flour was introduced by the Conquistadores...The celebration is an old-time Indian custom, sort of a Thanksgiving with acorns replacing turkeys...There will be demonstrations galore on how to knead the acorn into paste and then into soup or bread...Everything will be done in the old-fashioned way...Three Indian dance groups are scheduled to perform at 11 a.m., 3 p.m. and 8 p.m. each day. Sometimes the dancers get off to a late start in the morning, but the afternoon and evening schedules are usually on time...For sale will be a wide assortment of Indian homemade leather and bead belts, necklaces and bracelets...To round out the acorn food, there will be pit barbecued beef and, as a concession to the paleface, hot dogs and soft drinks..."

The little children in the Rancheria are bright and happy. The middle youth and young adults are taciturn. The older people are again bright and friendly, full of conversation about the Rancheria's future. In the unseen distance the sound of a hammer reverberates against the brush-covered hillside.

The Bureau of Indian Affairs estimates there are at least two thousand persons of either full, part or mixed (with other tribes) Miwok ancestry. The exact figure cannot be known because the vast majority of Miwok people are not now nor have they ever been associated with trust (reservation) lands.

The Tuolumne Rancheria has the greatest single concentration of Miwoks today -- 65 residents. The 323.1 acres are owned by a membership of approximately 140 tribesmen. A decade earlier, it had 46 residents.

Shingle Springs, a one-hundred-sixty acre rancheria in El Dorado County, has no residents, although some seventy-five to one hundred persons claim interest as descendants of the Miwok Indians for whom the land was purchased in 1916. Five people lived on this place ten years ago.

Two families of Miwok people live on the 330.66-acre Jackson Rancheria in Amador County.

Sheep Ranch, a .92-acre rancheria in Calaveras County, has one Miwok resident. Ten years ago, the population was three.

Four hundred of the estimated two thousand Miwoks live in the Yosemite area. Except for a few Public Domain allotments, the Federal Government did not set aside lands for Indians in that area -- hence, no reservations.

There is no official tribal roll of Miwok Indians. Many tribesmen have applied for inclusion on the California judgment funds roll. The cut-off date was September 21, 1968, the date the law was signed by the President.

The needs of the Miwok vary considerably. Many of the Miwok are quite self-sufficient and are as well off as their non-Indian neighbors.

The real problems, the Bureau of Indian Affairs says, are in the rural areas. "In this connection, their ills are similar to those of the non-Indian rural poor."

But, there is something more: there are cultural factors as well as elements of discrimination which yet inhibit economic progress of the Miwok.

Education is needed, but formal education alone is certainly not a panacea. There are some California Indian leaders who believe any "paternalistic-elitist reform or welfare programs which may subsequently be administered by the dominant population" tends not to ameliorate the life-style of a conquered people: apathetic, withdrawn, irresponsible, shy, lazy, etc.

Such programs, they argue, serve simply to reinforce a sense of inferiority and incapacity.

It may well be, these Indian leaders argue, that a conquered population can be truly liberated from the state of being conquered and powerless only through a process of self-liberation wherein the people in question acquire some significant measure of control over their own destiny. As a part of this process, a conquered people must acquire some control over the various mechanisms which serve to develop or to destroy that sense of personal inner security and pride which is essential for successful participation in socio-political affairs.

All forms of education, these Indian leaders argue, including those which derive from the home, the community, and mass media are crucial in this connection.

There is not much danger, however, that the socio-economic handouts of well-meaning "paternalistic-elitists" will have a crucially detrimental effect on the Miwok psyche. There simply isn't that much money being spent on these programs. A spokesman for the Bureau of Indian Affairs' Sacramento Area Office, which administers Miwok reservation affairs, states that the existing programs are "grossly underfunded for the needs that exist."

These programs, incidentally, are not geared to the Miwok Indians as a tribe. Rather, those services which are available, primarily in the education and employment assistance fields, are extended to qualified California Indians without regard to tribal affiliation.

Life goes on, and there are signs of progress. The Miwok will be swept along to better days together with the nation's other rural poor. The Federal Government's long-range policy seems to be a general raising of our economic basement.

The Miwok today do not (at least to white observers and friends) concern themselves overlong with the weightier ramifications of the psychological effects of exposure to racism. They talk about practical things: the digging of a well, the building of a house, a new school bus schedule.

They are not table-pounding orators decrying the loss of ancestral lands or the disruption of an ancient way of life. They are moved to action, however, by the desecration of Indian graves as allegedly took place recently on privately-owned land near Knight's Ferry.

A blue house trailer, unfancy and unyoung, jars the far view of the low, tree-studded hills that ring the Tuolumne Rancheria. But it is not hard to conjecture the way it might have been here in 1847 before the coming of the white man -- or even 1847 years before the birth of Christ, when the powerful fleets of the Greeks and the Phoenicians sacked and burned the cities of the rival Cretans.

The sky overhead and the light smoke- and pine-scented breeze coming down from the High Sierras is unchanged at Tuolumne. No doubt it was Coyote who has played this colossal joke on the People. He has opened a secret door to a race of men who combine the energy of the ant with the appetite of the bear.

But Coyote will be fooled by this joke. The Miwok are few -- but so are the coyotes. The Ant-Bear has destroyed both with equal efficiency.

Coyote has learned his lesson. He will begin playing other jokes that will fool the Ant-Bear. He has waited for the last moment when the People are nearly gone and the coyotes are nearly gone.

This will make the joke better.

It will work.

12

A Miwok Vocabulary

In 1908, the University of California published this vocabulary of Miwok words and dialects compiled by S. A. Barrett:

		Plains (N.W. Sierra)	Amador (N.E. Sierra)	Tuolumne (Cent. Sierra)	Mariposa (S. Sierra)	Bodega (W. Coast)	Marin (S. Coast)	Lake (N. Coast)
1	person	mïï-ko	miwû-k	míwu	míwu	ûla-mïtca ?	mïtca-kō	xōtsaxō
2	man	sawe	naña	naña	naña	tai	taiyis	tai
3	woman	ûsûï	osa	osa	oha	kûlêyi	kûlêyis	pōtsi
4	boy	salïnai	naña-tï	naña-tï	naña-tɕu	hêna	henas	hêna-pûtû
5	girl	ûmûnai	osa-tï	osa-tï	oha-tɕu	koya	kōya	kōla-pûtû
6	child		ehêlu	esellu	esellu			
7	infant	ōkï, pûnne	hiki-me	hiki-me	esellut-ki	ûtï	ûtï	pûtû
8	old man	ûtûm-tɕi	ûya-tï	ûya-na	humelet-ki	ōïyï	ōyis	nawa
9	old woman	ûtû-ya	ona-tï	on-oso	onotcōt-ki	kûyêyï	pōteis	hûkûyû
10	father	appa	upu	upu-tï	upu	əpï	apï	apï
11	mother	ûïka	uta	uta-tï	uta	ûnû	ûnû	ûnû
12	white man	ûûten-ko	allêni-k	ûyeayû	ōyeai	tōɕai	pōtōla-kō	ûtel-kō
13	head	tolo	hana	hana	hûkû	mōlû	mōlû	Lûbûdûk
14	hair	tolo	hana	yûse	hisok	mōlû-ñkatcen	kōlê-mōlû	sapa
15	eye	welai	suɾu	sûnɾu	huntu	sût	sût	sût
16	ear	coloto, alok	tokosu	tokosû	tolko	alōk	alōk	alōk
17	nose	hûûk	hûku	nïto	nïto	hûk	hûk	hûk
18	mouth	lûpe	awo	awo	awo	lakûm	lakûm	lûppe

	nepit	nepītʌ	nepirʌ	nepīr	lemtep	lemtip	letip
19 tongue	nepit	nepītʌ	nepirʌ	nepīr	lemtep	lemtip	letip
20 teeth	kʌt	kʌ́tʌ	kʌrʌ	kʌrʌ	gʌt	kʌt, gʌt	gʌt
21 neck	topa	topa	setce, lola	patcan, rawʌ	helēke	helēke	helēki
22 arm	tawa, tumal	tʌmalu	woñotū	tissʌ, ūkʌs	talīk	taūlī	taūlīk
23 hand	ekʌ	ukusʌ, tissʌ	tissʌ	tissū	ūkū	ūkūs	ūkū
24 fingers	kitcayi	tcīgola	tissʌ	tissu	ūkū	ūkūs	kūpūm
25 nails	ti	tissū	sala	mūsū	pītci	pītci	.ti
26 breasts (female)	mū'	mūsū	mūsū		mū	mū	mū
27 milk	mū'	mūsū	mūsū		ewe	ewe	
28 knee	honoi	hoñoyū	hoñoyū	hoñoi	mōwi	mōwi	tokōllō
29 leg	tʌna	tuñu, kawali	tuñu, hotcanū	tuñu	hol	etca, hol	lōlō
30 foot	kolo	hate, kolo	hate	hate	ko	ko, kōyo	kōllō
31 bone	wūski	kutcʌutcʌ	ku'tcutcu	kutcute	mʌtci	kūlūm	kūlūm
32 rib		woto	wīma	alaka	wīpīk	wīpīk	hatsi
33 blood	kitcaū	kītcaūñ	kītcawʌ	kītcaū	kītcaū	kītcaū	kītsaū
34 excrement	kʌna	kūnatʌ	kūnatūs	kʌnat			
35 chief	tceka	haiapu	haiapō	haiapō	hōipū	hōipūs	hōipū
36 doctor	ūmise	alīni	alīni[25]	rūyūk	temnepʌ	wenen-apī	yōmta
37 friend	otta	sake-t	moe, aiyu-t	otci-nti, aiyu-ntiōiya		ōiam-gō	ōiya
38 house	kōdja	kōtca	kōtca, ūtcū	ūtcū	kōtca	kōtca	wēyi
39 door	ūkūya	ōlatʌ	ūkūya	ūkūya	ka	ka	ka
40 dance-house	hanēpū	hañi	hañi	hañi	lʌmma	lamma	lamma
41 bow	tanʌka	kutca	kutca, sollokū	yawe	konō	kōno	kōnō
42 arrow	haīlo	yatci	paipū	mutckū	lanta	lanta	kiūwa
43 knife	satakū	kītce	kniaiyi	sope	hūlaia	hūlaia	tsitsa
44 boat	saga	saku	saku	wore	saka	saka	nū
45 string		lʌkabʌnʌ	īmasi	hīlo	katteen	katteen	cūtsa
46 pipe	topokela	paūmma	paūmma	paūmma	sūgūlūpū	sūmki	cūmkit-tūmai
47 tobacco	kasū	kasū	kasʌ	kahʌ	kaiyaū	kaiyaū	kaiyaū
48 awl	lʌya	tcʌlla	tcʌlla	tcʌlla	līisaya	mōōi, sutaya	hūtik

109

	Plains (N.W. Sierra)	Amador (N.E. Sierra)	Tuolumne (Cent. Sierra)	Mariposa (S. Sierra)	Bodega (W. Coast)	Marin (S. Coast)	Lake (N. Coast)
49 burden basket			tcĭkele	tcĭkele	tika	tika	tika
50 cradle	hōpa		hiki	hiki	saka	saka	tŭnĭk
51 pestle		kawatci	kawatcĭ	kawatcĭ	pa	paiya, pa	tōwai
52 comb			sakanĭ	sakanĭ	γatcek	sōnēk	lawine
53 mush paddle	salakka	talōwa	[not used]	[not used]		wĭwĭl	ōlak
54 mush stirrer	[not used]	sawaiya	sʋwaiya	sʋwaiya	[not used]	[not used]	[not used]
55 sun	hi	hĭēma	hĭēma	watʋ	hi	hi	hĭ, hĭntaka
56 moon	kōme	kōme	kōme	kōme	pŭlŭlŭk	pŭlŭlŭk	kŭmēnawa
57 star	holokai	hosokōna	hosōkōna	tcalaʈŭ	hitĭ	hitĭs	tōle
58 day	hĭama	hĭēma	hĭēma	hĭēma	hi	hiana	hĭ
59 night	kawŭl	kawʋlu	kawʋlu	kawʋlu-ʈo	kawŭl	kawŭl	kawŭl
60 wind	wŭlŭlĭ	hena	hena	kanʋma	kĭwel	hena, kĭwel	hena
61 thunder	lĭlik	timele	timeleli	timeleli	talawa	talawa	talawa
62 rain	hōma	nuka	nuka	nʋka, ŭmŭtca	ŭpa	ŭpa	ŭpa
63 snow	kela	kela	kela	kela	yawem	yawem	tana
64 fire	wŭke	wuke	wuke	wʋke, hʋyŭ	wĭkĭ	wŭki	wĭki
65 smoke	kali	hakisʋ	hakisʋ	hakisa	kal	kal	kal
66 ashes	sike	yōlĭ	yōmĭ, sike	sĭke	yemĭ	yemĭ	wilōk
67 water	kĭk	kĭkŭ	kĭkʋ	kĭkʋ	lĭwa	kĭk, lĭwa	kĭk
68 earth, dirt	γotok	walli	walli	walli	yōa	yōa	yōwa
69 earth, world	walli	walli	walli	walli	wēa	wēa	walli
70 stream	wakatce	wakalŭ	wakalʋ[28]	wakal-mŭʈo	tcok	tcok	wŭwe
71 valley	wiskapa	pʋlaiʋ	pʋlaiʋ	aiyi	loklo	lokla	lōklō
72 mountain	wēpa	hĭsŭ-wit	leme, hĭsŭm	leme	paiyĭ	paiyĭs	pawi
73 rock	sawa	sawa	sʋwa	hawa	lŭppŭ	lŭpŭ	lŭpŭ
74 tree	alawa	lēka	lama	lama	aĭwa	alwas	alwa
75 wood	tŭmai	sŭsŭ	susu	huhu	tūmai	tūmai	tūmai
76 white oak	sĭwek	molla	lēka	lēka		ŭlĭkĭ	mŭle

110

No.	English							
77	black oak	sasa	sasa	telēli	telēli	kȯtin	kȯtis	ūte
78	manzanita[31]	ēye	ēye	eye	eye	eyi	tsilaka	ēyi
79	medicine	wene	wene	hūsiku	loha	wene	wene	
80	poison	tūpele	tūpülla	yenʊwa	yenpa	patca	patca	haūwi
81	acorn	otcapa	wīlisa	mɨyʉ, telēli	mɨyʉ, telēli	ūmpa	ūmpa	waiya
82	mush	pītca	nʉpa	nʉpa	nʉpa-ti	ūlki	ūlki	ūlki
83	pinole, meal	tūyü	tūyü	tūyü	tūyü	ūskün	ūskūi	ūskün
84	bread		ūle, yoko	ule	ule			
85	whiskey		[Spanish]	[Spanish]	[Spanish]	ūmū-līwa	ōmū-līwa	xaixaigʻik
86	meat	ümēna	hūkü	pītcēma	pītcēma	tcoyeke	kesūm	sūki
87	dog	tcītcü	tcukü	tcukü	tcukü	haiyūsa	haiyūsa	
88	grizzly bear	usumati	usumati	usumati	ʊhʉmati	kūle	kūle	kūle
89	coyote	ōleti	oletcü	aseli[a]	alēli	ȯye	ȯye	ōle
90	deer	uwüya	uwuya	uwüya	uwüya, hika	tcōyeke	kesūm-ala-kesūm	sūki
91	jack rabbit	epali	eplali	eplali	eplali	tcamī	aūle	tsamī
92	rabbit skin robe	ūdjüle	yūpte	yūptí	yūptí, ʈoli	mēye	mēye	mele
93	bird	tcītcipuk	mitcematī?	tcītcka	tcītcka	ȯyēkēya	ekēya	hūs
94	buzzard	tcʊhʉ	tcūhü	hūusū	hūhū	sokotok	kekekai	tsȯkȯkȯ
95	quail (valley)	nʊkute	hekeke	hekeke	hekeke	saiyite	saiyite	caiyîts
96	bluejay (valley)	saiisi	taiti	taismū	taitcü	kūlup'pī		
97	humming bird	kulūlü	litcitci	litcitci	litcitci	ȯyewōlōlōk		
98	yellow hammer	tiiwai	tiwaiu	tiwaiu	tiwai	panak	wolōlak	tsiyak
99	red-head w'pecker	paltina	palatata	palatata	palatata	melēya	palatcak	panak
100	turtle	awannai	awannata	awannata	awanta	kotola	melēya	melēya
101	frog		wataksaiyi	wataksaiyi	watakʊna		kotola	kȯlȯlȯ
102	rattlesnake	tcatakaʀa	wakali	lawaʈi	lawaʈi	kiʈakwakaklai	ūkūlis	hȯlȯmai
103	fish	pü	lapisaiyu	lapisai	lapisai	elēwi	lota	kats
104	salmon	tūkün	kūkünü	kosūm	kosūm	kasi	kasi	kassi

111

		Plains (N.W. Sierra)	Amador (N.E. Sierra)	Tuolumne (Cent. Sierra)	Mariposa (S. Sierra)	Bodega (W. Coast)	Marin (S. Coast)	Lake (N. Coast)
105	louse	ken	ketu	keru, teupsi	keṛu, lupsi	ket	teupsi	ket
106	flea	kîḳî	kukusu	kukusu	kuku	kîḳî	kûḳûs	kîḳî
107	mosquito	ûyîgûgî	uyukusu	uyukusu	teulu	soiyō	soiyō	soiyō
108	grasshopper	kodjo	kotco	kotco	añût	kotok	koto	kōtō
109	yellowjacket	sûsû	melñaiñ	melñaiu	melñai	menani	menani	mēnani
110	white	pntûtu	keleli	keleli	pasassi	potōta	pōṭōla	tsetaû
111	black	kûlûlû	kûlûlî	kûlûlî	Tûxûxi	lōkota	mûlûta	mûlûmûlû
112	red	wûtete	weteti	weteti[34]	yōtcotci	kiteûlû	ûlûta	awaaawa
113	large	teme	utû	ututî	oyani	ōmotak	ûnûni	ûdi
114	small	itîti	îtcibiti	Tûnitci	tcinimiteu	ûmûtce	ûti	kûcci
115	good	welwel	kûdjî	kutci	teuṛu	tōwi	tōwis	emēne
116	bad	saiye	saiye	usûtu	uswî, uxutuma	ōmû	ōmû	ōbû
117	sweet	tcûtcûî	teûdjûyû	tcûya	tcûyeña	kōįyûp	kawatcû	kōikōi
118	north	tala-wit	taman	tamalin	tamalin	kani	kan-win	kanin
119	east	hûke-wit	hîsû-wit	hisum	hîhûm	ala	hinhine	ala
120	south	yakû-wit	tcûmutc	tcûmetc	tcûmetc	ōlom, olōm	ōlōp	ōlōm-wali
121	west	etca-wit	olō-wit	olo-win	olo-win	helwa	helwaia	ōlōm ?
122	up	newit (hîgu)	lîle	lîle	lîle	lîle	lîle	lîle
123	down	wanit	walim, tamma	wallim	wallim, hûye	hōime	hōime	wēa
124	no	hela	ewutî	ewuṛu	ken	hûma	hûma	hella
125	yes	hûî	hu	hu	huu	û	û	û
126	one	kenatu	lûti	keñe	keñe	kenne	kenne	kenne
127	two	oyoko	ōtiko	ōtiko	otiko	osa	ossa	ōtta
128	three	teloko	tolokou	tolokosu	Tolokot	telēga	telēka	telēka
129	four	ōyîseko	oyîsa	oyîsa	ōyîsa	lûya	hûya	ōtōta
130	five	kasoko	masōka	masoka	mahōka	kennekû	kenekûs	kedekkō
131	six	temepu	temōka	temōka	Temōka	patcîtak	patcîtak	patsadat
132	seven	kenekak	kenekagû	kenekagu	titawa	sēlawî	semlawi	cemlawi

112

#	English	kawenta	kawinta	kawinta	ōssüwa	ōsüya	ōttaia
133	eight	kawenta	kawinta	kawinta	ōssüwa	ōsüya	ōttaia
134	nine	wõe	woe	elĩwa	kennekoʈo	ūnūtas	kenenhēlak
135	ten	ekūye	naatca	naatea	kitci, gĩtci	kĩtsis	ūkūkūlsi
136	eleven	lūsa-kena	keñ-heteagᵤ	naatca-keñe-hateenï	kenne-wallik	kenne-lĩlek	kenne-wallik
137	twenty	naa	naa	ōtiak-naatca	osa-gĩtci	ōsa-gĩtcis	ōtta-ʈūmai
138	eat	uwᵤ	uwᵤ	uwᵤ	yōlūm		yōlūm
139	drink	ūhū	ūsu	uhū	ūssū		ūssū
140	run	hᵤwate	kūwaʈu	hᵤwaʈe	hicwate		hitsū
141	dance	kalʈe	kalañᵤ	kalañe	kawūl		laki
142	sing	mᵤli-nī	mᵤli-nī	ūmaʈe, mᵤlina	koya		kōya
143	shoot	añke	tᵤmkᵤ	tuke	tūwe		tūwen
144	kill	yena-ni	yᵤna-ni	yehe	ōke		katten
145	shout	kawūñe-ni	kauñe-ni	kᵤwa-k	lūtū		haiyap

13

Miwok Village Sites

The Bureau of American Ethnology lists the following Miwok villages and their locations:

PLAINS MIWOK

Chuyumkatat, Mayeman, Mokoe-umni, Sukididi, Supu, Tukui, and Yomit -- all placed on the Cosumnes River.

Hulpu-mni -- on the east bank of the Sacramento River below Sacramento.

Lel-amni, Mokel(-umni), and Sakayak-umni -- all on the Mokelumne River.

Lulimal, Umucha, and Yumhui -- all near the Cosumnes River.

Ochech-ak -- on Jackson Creek.

NORTHERN MIWOK

Apautawilu, and Ketina -- between the Mokelumne and Calaveras Rivers.

Chakane-su, Seweu-su, and Yuloni -- on Jackson Creek.

Kechenu, and Kaitimu -- at the head of the Calaveras River.

Heina -- between the Mokelumne River and the head of the Calaveras River.

Huta-su -- at San Andreas.

Kunusu -- near the Mokelumne River.

Mona-su -- on the headwaters of the Calaveras River.

Noma, and Omo -- near the South Fork of the Cosumnes River.

Penken-su -- inland south of the Mokelumne River.

Pola-su -- near Jackson.

Sopochi -- between the Mokelumne River and Jackson Creek.

Tukupe-su -- at Jackson.

Tumuti -- on the headwaters of Jackson Creek.

Upusuni -- on the Mokelumne River.

Yule -- south of the Cosumnes River.

CENTRAL MIWOK

Akankau-nchi -- two towns of this name -- one near Sonora; the other a considerable distance to the southwest.

Akawila -- between a branch of the Tuolumne River and the Stanislaus River.

Akutanuka -- northwest of the Stanislaus River.

Alakani, and Sasamu -- east of San Andreas.

Shulaputi -- just southeast of Sasamu.

Chakachi-no, Kapanina, and Suchumumu -- southwest of Sonora.

Sopka-su -- southwest of Sonora between the Stanislaus and Tuolumne Rivers.

Waka-che -- southwest of and near Sonora.

Hangwite, Sutamasina, and Wokachet -- on the south fork of the Stanislaus River.

Hechhechi (from which the San Francisco aqueduct is named) -- on the headwaters of the Tuolumne River.

Hochhochmeti -- on the Tuolumne River.

Pasi-nu -- on the Tuolumne River southeast of Sonora.

Humata, and Katuka -- on a branch of the Calaveras River.

Hunga, Telese-no, Telula, and Tunuk-chi -- northeast of Sonora.

Kawinucha -- near the north fork of the Stanislaus River.

Kesa -- a short distance east of Sonora.

Olawiye, and Sukwela -- east of Sonora.

Kewe-no, Tipotoya, Tulana-chi, Tuyiwu-nu, Oloikoto, and Wuyu -- on the Stanislaus River.

Kosoimuno-nu -- between the Stanislaus River and San Andreas.

Kotoplans and Pokto-no -- a short distance west of Sonora.

Kulamu -- on a branch of the Tuolumne River.

Pangasema-nu -- on a northern branch of the Tuolumne River.

Singawu-nu -- at the head of a branch of the Tuolumne River.

Kuluti -- at Sonora.

Loyowisa -- near the junction of the Middle and South forks of the Stanislaus River.

Wolanga-su -- south of the junction between the South and Middle forks of the Stanislaus River.

Yungakatok -- near the junction of the North and Middle forks of the Stanislaus River.

Newichu -- between the Stanislaus River and a head branch of the Calaveras River.

Pigliku (the Miwok pronunciation of ''Big Creek'') -- south of the Tuolumne River.

Sala -- just south of Pigliku.

Pota -- a short distance northwest of Sonora.

Siksike-no -- south of Sonora near the Tuolumne River.

Sukanola -- southeast of Sonora.

Takema -- on the Middle Fork of the Stanislaus River.

Tulsuna -- between the South and Middle forks of the Stanislaus River.

SOUTHERN MIWOK

Alaula-chi, Angisawepa, Awal, Hikena, Kakahula-chi, Kitiwana, Kuyuka-chi, Owelinhatihu, Siso-chi, Wilito, and Yawoka-chi -- all on the Merced River.

Awani -- close to Yosemite.

Kasumati, and Nochu-chi -- near Mariposa.

Nowach, and Olwia -- on the headwater of the Chowchilla River.

Palachan, and Sotpok -- on a southern branch of the Merced River.

Sayangasi -- between the middle courses of the Merced and Tuolumne Rivers.

Sope-nchi -- on a northern branch of the Merced River.

Wasema -- near the head of the Fresno River.

Wehilto -- on the upper waters of the Fresno River.

According to ethnologists, many other Miwok village names have been recorded, but the above list contains all those which are well authenticated as independent settlements.

14

Bibliography

MIWOK SOURCES

Aginsky, B.W., "Central Sierra", *UofC Anthro. Records, Vol. 8,* Berkeley, 1943.

Angulo, J. de and Freeland, L.S., "Miwok and Pomo Myths", *Journal of Amer. Folklore, Vol. 41,* Boston, New York, 1928.

Angulo, J. de and Harcourt, B. d', "La musique des Indiens de la California du Nord", *Journal de la Societe des Americanistes, Vol. 23,* Paris, 1931.

Bancroft, Hubert Howe, *The Native Races of the Pacific States,* New York, 1875.

Barrett, S.A., "The Geography and Dialects of the Miwok Indians", *UofC Publications in Amer. Arch. and Ethn., Vol. 6,* Berkeley, 1908.
"Totemism Among the Miwok Indians", *Jour. of Amer. Folk-Lore, Vol. 21,* Boston, New York, 1908.
"Myths of the Southern Sierra Miwok", *UofC Publications in Amer. Arch. and Ethn., Vol. 16,* Berkeley, 1919.

Barrett, S.A. and Gifford, E.W., "Miwok Material Culture", *Bulletins of the Public Museum of the City of Milwaukee, Vol. 2,* Milwaukee, 1933.

Beeler, M.S., "Saclan", *International Jour. of Amer. Linguistics, XXI,* New York, 1955.

Bingaman, John W., *The Ahwahneechees--A Story of Yosemite Indians,* Palm Springs, 1966.

Broadbent, Sylvia, "The Southern Sierra Miwok Language", *UofC Pub. in Linguistics, Vol. 38,* Berkeley, 1964.

Buckbee, Edna Bryan, *The Saga of Old Tuolumne,* New York, 1935.

Bunnell, L.H., *Discovery of the Yosemite,* 1880.

Christman, Enos, *One Man's Gold,* New York, 1930.

Clark, C.U., "Excerpts from the Journals of Prince Paul of Wurtemberg, Year 1850", *SW Journal of Anthro.*, *XV,* Albuquerque, 1959.

Clark, G., *Indians of the Yosemite Valley and Vicinity,* Yosemite, 1904.

Cook, Sherburne F., "The Conflict Between the California Indians and White Civilization", *UofC Pub. in Ibero-Americana,* Berkeley, 1943. "The Aboriginal Population of the San Joaquin Valley", *Calif. Anthro. Records, XVI,* Berkeley, 1955. "The Aboriginal Population of the North Coast of California", *Anthro. Records, XVI,* Berkeley, 1956. "The Aboriginal Population of Alameda and Contra Costa Counties", *Calif. Anthro. Records, XVI,* Berkeley, 1957.

Curtis, E.S., *The North American Indian, Vol. 14,* Norwood, 1924.

Davis, James, "Trade Routes and Economic Exchange Among the Indians of California", *UofC Arch. Research Facility Survey No. 54,* Berkeley, 1961.

Dixon, R.B. and Kroeber, A.L., "New Linguistic Families in California", *Amer. Anthro., Vol. 15,* New York, Lancaster, Menasha, 1913.

Driver, Harold Edson, *Indians of North America,* Chicago, 1961.

Farquhar, Francis P., *History of the Sierra Nevada,* Berkeley, 1966.

Freeland, L.S., "Language of the Sierra Miwok", *Indiana U. Pub. in Anthro. and Linguistics, VI,* 1951.

Freeland, L.S. and Broadbent, Sylvia, *Central Sierra Miwok Dictionary,* Berkeley, 1960.

Gifford, E.W., "Miwok Moieties", *UofC Pub. in Amer. Arch. and Ethn., Vol. 12,* Berkeley, 1916. "Miwok Myths", *UofC Pub. in Amer. Arch. and Ethn., Vol. 12,* Berkeley, 1917. "California Kinship Terminologies", *UofC Pub. in Amer. Arch. and Ethn., Vol. 18,* Berkeley, 1922. "California Anthropometry", *UofC Pub. in Amer. Arch. and Ethn., Vol. 22,* Berkeley, 1926. "Miwok Cults", *UofC Pub. in Amer. Arch. and Ethn., Vol. 18,* Berkeley, 1926. "Miwok Lineages and the Political Unit in Aboriginal California", *Amer. Anthropologist, Vol. 28,* Washington, New York, Lancaster, Menasha, 1926. "Miwok Lineages", *Amer. Anthropologist, Vol. 46,* Washington, New York, Lancaster, Menasha, 1944. "Central Miwok Ceremonies", *Anthropological Records, XIV,* Berkeley, 1955.

BIBLIOGRAPHY

Gifford, Edward and Block, Gwendoline, *California Night Entertainments,* Glendale, 1930.

Heizer, Robert Fleming, *Language, Territories and Names of California Indian Tribes,* Berkeley, 1906.
The California Indians, Berkeley, 1951.
"Some Archaeological Sites and Cultures of the Central Sierra Nevada", *UofC Arch. Survey No. 21,* Berkeley, 1953.

Henshaw, H.W. and Kroeber, A.L., "Moquelumnan Family", *Bulletins of the Bur. of Amer. Ethn., Vol. 30,* Washington, 1907.

Hodge, Frederick, "Handbook of American Indians", *Bur. of Amer. Ethn. Bulletin 30,* Washington, 1907.

Holmes, W.H., "Anthropological Studies in California", *Report for the U. S. National Museum,* Washington, 1900.

Hutchings, J.M., *In the Heart of the Sierras,* Oakland, 1883.

Kroeber, A.L., "The Dialectic Divisions of the Moquelumnan Family", *Amer. Anthro., Vol. 12,* Washington, New York, Lancaster, Menasha, 1906.
"Indian Myths of South Central California", *UofC Pub. in Amer. Arch. and Ethn., Vol. 4,* Berkeley, 1907.
"On the Evidences of the Occupation of Certain Regions by the Miwok Indians", *UofC Pub. in Amer. Arch. and Ethn., Vol. 6,* Berkeley, 1908.
"The Languages of the Coast of California North of San Francisco", *UofC Pub. in Amer. Arch. and Ethn., Vol. 9,* Berkeley, 1911.
Cultural and Natural Areas of Native North America, Berkeley, 1913.
"California Place Names of Indian Origin", *UofC Pub. in Amer. Arch. and Ethn.,* Berkeley, 1916.
"California Kinship Systems", *UofC Pub. in Amer. Arch. and Ethn., Vol. 12,* Berkeley, 1917.
California Culture Provinces, Berkeley, 1920.
"Handbook of the Indians of California", *Bulletins of the Bureau of Amer. Ethn., Vol. 78,* Washington, 1925.
"The Nature of Land Holding Groups", *UofC Arch. Research Facility,* Berkeley, 1961.

Kroeber, Theodora, *Ishi In Two Worlds,* Berkeley, 1969.

Lillard, J.B. and Purves, W.K., "The Archaeology of the Deer Creek - Cosumnes Area", *Sacramento Jr. College Dept. of Anthro. Bulletin, 1,* Sacramento, 1936.

Loeb, E.M., "The Western Kuksu Cult", *UofC Pub. in Amer. Arch. and Ethn.,* Berkeley, 1932.

119

Merriam, C.H., "Distribution and Classifications of the Mewan Stock", *Amer. Anthro., Vol. 9,* Washington, Lancaster, New York, Menasha, 1907.
"Totemism in California", *American Anthropologist, Vol. 10,* Washington, 1908.
The Dawn of the World, Cleveland, 1910.
Distribution of Indian Tribes in the Southern Sierra and Adjacent Parts of the San Joaquin Valley, California, Science, 1914.
"Indian Village and Camp Sites in Yosemite Valley", *Sierra Club Bulletins, Vol. 10,* 1917.
Studies of California Indians, Ed. by Dept. of Anthro., UofC Berkeley, 1955.

Merrill, Ruth Earl, "Plants Used in Basketry by the California Indians", *UofC Pub. in Arch. and Ethn.,* Berkeley, 1923.

Mooney, J., "Notes on the Cosumnes Tribes", *Amer. Anthro.,* Vol. 3, Washington, 1890.

Paden, Irene and Schlichtmann, Margaret, *The Big Oak Flat Road to Yosemite,* Yosemite, 1959.

Perkins, William, *Journal of Life at Sonora, 1849-1852,* Berkeley, 1964.

Powers, S., "The California Indians", *Overland Monthly, Vol. 10,* San Francisco, 1873.
"Tribes of California", *U.S. Geographical and Geological Survey of the Rocky Mountain Region, Vol. 3,* Washington, 1877.

Riley, J.H. "Vocabulary of the Kah-we-Yak and Kah-so-wah Indians", *Historical Magazine, Vol. 3,* Boston, New York, Morrisania, 1868.

Russell, Carl P., *One Hundred Years in Yosemite,* Yosemite, 1957.

Schenck, W.E., "Historic Aboriginal Groups of the California Delta Region", *UofC Pub. of the Amer. Arch. and Ethn., Vol. 23,* Berkeley, 1926.

Schenck, W.E. and Dawson, J., "Archaeology of the Northern San Joaquin Valley", *UofC Pub. in Amer. Arch. and Ethn., Vol. 25,* Berkeley, 1929.

Schmidt, W., *Die Miwok. Die Ursprung der Gottesidee, II,* Munster, I. W., 1929-34.

Shafer R., "Penutian", *Inter. Journal of Amer. Linguistics, Vol. 13,* New York, 1947.

Smith, E.S., *Po-ho-no and the Legends of the Yosemite,* Carmel, 1927.

BIBLIOGRAPHY

Squier, R.S., "The Manufacture of Flint Implements By the Indians of Northern and Central California", *UofC Arch. Survey*, Berkeley, 1953.

Swanton, John R., "The Indian Tribes of North America", *Bureau of Amer. Ethn., Bulletin 145*, Washington, 1952.

Taylor, Mrs. H.J., *Yosemite Indians and Other Sketches*, San Francisco, 1936.

Wallace, William, "The Archaeological Deposit in Moaning Cave, Calaveras County", *UofC Arch. Survey No. 12*, Berkeley, 1951.

Wissler, Clark, *The American Indian*, Oxford, 1922.

SECONDARY SOURCES

(These sources may or may not contain specific Miwok references, but are included as sources used to shed light on the Miwok as a California aborigine.)
Bolton, Herbert E., *Coronado On the Turquoise Trail*, Albuquerque, 1949.

Bruff, J. Goldsborough, *Journals, Drawings and Other Papers, April 2, 1849 - July 20, 1851*, New York, 1949.
California State Legislature, *Journals*, Sacramento, 1851.

Clark, William B., "Gold Districts of California", *Calif. Div. of Mines and Geology, Bulletin 193*, San Francisco, 1970.

Culin, Stewart, "Games of the North American Indians", *Bureau of Amer. Ethn. Annual Report*, Washington, 1907.

Curtin, Jeremiah,*Creation Myths of Primitive America*, Boston, 1898.

Dunne, Peter Masten, *Black Robes of California*, Berkeley, 1952.

Emerson, Ellen Russell, *Indian Myths*, Minneapolis, 1965.

Fages, Pedro, *A Historical, Political and Natural Description of California*, Berkeley, 1937.

Grinnell, Joseph and Storer, Tracy Irwin, *Life Zones of the Yosemite Regions*, New York, 1921.

Grunsky, Carl Edward, *Stockton Boyhood*, Berkeley, 1959.

Gudde, Erwin, *California Place Names*, Berkeley, 1969.

Heap, Gwinn Harris, *Central Route to the Pacific*, Glendale, 1957.

Hittell, Theodore H., *History of California*, San Francisco, 1897.

James, Harry, *The Cahuilla Indians*, Los Angeles, 1960.

Judson, Katharine Berry, *Myths and Legends of California and Old Southwest,* Chicago, 1912.

Muir, John, *Mountains of California,* New York, 1917.

Olmsted, R.R., *Scenes of Wonder and Curiosity From Hutchings' California Magazine (1856-61),* Berkeley, 1962.

Robinson W.W., *Land In California,* Berkeley, 1948.

Sharfman, Dr. I. Harold, *Nothing Left to Commemorate,* Glendale, 1969.

Taylor, Bayard, *Eldorado,* New York, 1850.

U.S. Bureau of the Census, *Indian Population in the U.S.,* Washington, 1910.

Index

Fauna

Flora

Institutions

Life

Material

People

Index

Places

Spiritual

Index

Let's Play Peek-a-Boo

By Joan Webb
Illustrated by Kim Mulkey

GOLDEN PRESS • NEW YORK
Western Publishing Company, Inc., Racine, Wisconsin

Text copyright © 1981 by Western Publishing Company, Inc. Illustrations copyright © 1981 by Kim Mulkey.
All rights reserved. Printed in the U.S.A. No part of this book may be reproduced or copied in any form without
written permission from the publisher. GOLDEN®, A FIRST LITTLE GOLDEN BOOK, and GOLDEN PRESS®
are trademarks of Western Publishing Company, Inc. Library of Congress Catalog Card Number: 80-85082
ISBN 0-307-10109-6/ISBN 0-307-68109-2 (lib. bdg.)   B C D E F G H I J

Sarah and her brother Tim like to play games.
They play pat-a-cake,

and follow-the-leader,

and "How big are you?"

But Sarah's favorite game
is peek-a-boo.

They hide behind the door

and play peek-a-boo with Mommy.

They hide behind the chair

and play peek-a-boo with puppy.

They play peek-a-boo at bedtime.

They play peek-a-boo outside.

Daddy likes to play. . .

and Grandpa likes to play.

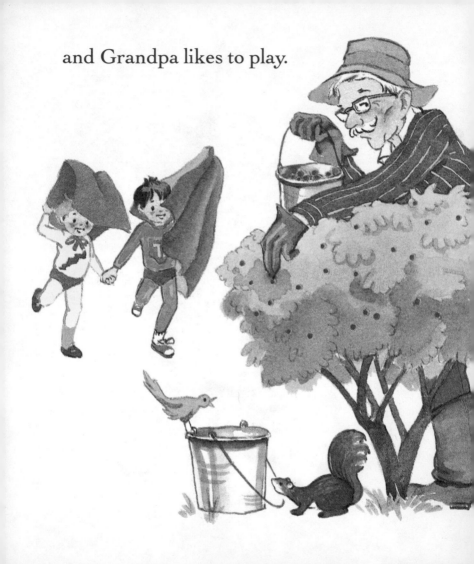

Would you like to play, too?

Can you find Sarah and Tim?

Now where are they hiding?

Can you find them? Look and see.

Peek-a-boo here and peek-a-boo there,
it's fun to play peek-a-boo everywhere!